Rodney Collins

THE
WORLD
THAT
IS

B. F. KURZWEG

CONCORDIA
PUBLISHING
HOUSE
SAINT LOUIS

CONCORDIA PUBLISHING HOUSE, ST. LOUIS, MISSOURI

CONCORDIA PUBLISHING HOUSE LTD., LONDON, W. C. 1

© 1965 BY CONCORDIA PUBLISHING HOUSE

LIBRARY OF CONGRESS CATALOG CARD NO. 65-16964

MANUFACTURED IN THE UNITED STATES OF AMERICA

PREFACE

This little book suggests a theological approach to Christian life in the world. It takes the world seriously as the creation of God and the sphere of His redeeming and preserving activity.

With Martin Luther this volume views Christian ethics as the living out of a man's Christian faith. Sometimes church members have been tempted to forget this dynamic interpretation of Christian theology, with its emphasis on the intimate relationship between faith and life. The valuable Reformation distinction between justification and sanctification has been in danger of becoming a divorce. Christians need to be reminded that God would propel their lives by the dynamic of His forgiving love in Christ. The Christian life is faith realizing itself in love.

The vast amount of recent Luther research is discovering the relevance of the Reformer's deep insight into the message of the Scriptures and the nature of the Christian faith. Luther is speaking today with new significance. His distinction between Law and Gospel, with its meaningful application to the Christian in society, is being heard. His emphasis on the Word of God as the powerful message of God's judgment and redemption of mankind is again being taken seriously.

It is presumptuous to attempt an adequate approach to Christian ethics in the short space of this book. Such brevity may easily lead to misrepresentation and misunderstanding. The reader is requested to take this factor into consideration. Other volumes of this series will explore the application of principles herein contained to the various structures of human existence. They will spell out in greater detail the tension in the Christian's life between old and new, between flesh and spirit, between present and future. They will apply Law and Gospel to the specific areas of Christian man's relationship to God's world.

It is my hope that the reader of this volume may be led to a deeper appreciation of his place in God's world and to a greater realization of his responsibility in Christ Jesus.

B. F. KURZWEG

Epiphany 1965

CONTENTS

1

MAN'S WORLD

Through the ages men have tried to formulate their views of the world in which they live. They have tried to describe man's mysterious relationship to the world by meaningful theories and observations. They have tried to find one central pivot around which to range the whole gamut of human experience.

The World of Nature

Many of these attempts have stressed the world of nature. The concepts of time and space, for example, have served as possible pivots in explaining man's relationship to his world. The ancient Greeks saw the world and man as part of an endless repetition of time. To live and to die was considered to be an inevitable phenomenon of the eternal wheels of time and fate.

Today our concern rests with space. Ever since it

came to be commonly accepted that the earth is not the center of the universe, man's attention has turned to the mysteries of spatial relationships. Man is seen as part of a limitless expanse, living out his life as an insignificant being on an insignificant planet in an insignificant "corner" of infinite space.

When man's relationship to the world is viewed solely in terms of time and space, he becomes a rather impersonal being. His life is determined by mysterious and unknowable forces beyond his control. He is subject to the world of nature.

People have tried to explain their relationship to this world of nature in various ways. Some have said that it is governed by spiritual forces. Others deny the existence of any spiritual powers. For them life consists in the movement of matter, the coming together and pulling apart of atoms.

Materialistic world views, for example, say that life is simply the emergence of one body over others. Biological world views see life as a process in which the individual is more or less an accident of nature. What a man says or does is determined by his heredity and climatic environment. From this latter view have sprouted social, political, and economic theories — all of them attempting to explain the relationship of men to the world and to one another.

Underlying these views of man and his world during the past several centuries is the so-called scientific method. This has become for modern man the way by which he understands his world. Up through the Middle Ages men interpreted their world through the eyes of philosophy and religion. During the time from Francis Bacon to the Enlightenment this changed. Ever since the beginning of the modern age several centuries ago, man understands his world much differently. He sees it in terms of a continuous process operating according to unchangeable universal laws.

This new outlook on life has influenced every one of us. We live in the scientific age. We share its discoveries. We turn on light switches in our homes with the confidence that they will cause lights to go on. If they don't work, we are quite sure they can be fixed. We have decided convictions about the accomplishments of the scientific method.

Important in the scientific approach to the world is its interest in observable facts. It is concerned with what can be seen and proved. This approach has affected every area of man's knowledge and life, including his religious beliefs. We no longer accept some statement as true simply because an authority in government or church tells us it is true. In this we are different from the people of the prescientific age. We are also aware that the facts quite repeatedly let us down. "Don't confuse me with the facts" is a humorous expression, but it says something about man's modern dilemma. We have come to have great respect for the facts. But difficulties arise when we are faced with conflicting claims regarding fact. Who is right? Which theory regarding man's relationship to his world is correct? Which theory of government or economics provides the right answer? What beliefs regarding life and death are substantiated by the facts?

This is the dilemma of modern man. He has come to regard only the scientific and the factual as meaningful, but he is becoming more and more aware that there is no clearcut way to determine the factual. In former days truth could be pinned down to certain intellectual facts pronounced by authorities in state or church. Today this has changed. Modern education no longer tells people *what* to think but *how* to think. Modern advertising is careful not to tell people what they must accept but leads them by means of flattery and repetition to "think for themselves."

In this confusion of conflicting theories and ideas about life, modern man is looking for truth and security. It is the nature of man to want to have something which he regards as true on which to build his life. Unless he has such a center around which to structure his experiences, life is fragmented and meaningless. Modern Americans know so much about so many things, but many of them are emotionally and mentally confused because all of their knowledge and experience seems to have no center and therefore no meaning.

All of us are affected by the modern theories regarding man and his world. We know that in terms of space we are a most insignificant speck on a most insignificant planet of a seemingly limitless universe. We agree with that emphasis of physics which says matter is constantly undergoing change. We agree with that emphasis of biology which says we are influenced by heredity. We agree with those theories which say we are influenced by our climatic environment. We use the scientific method every day of our lives. We are the children of our age.

But a problem arises when any one of these theories claims to be the center of our existence. We are willing to borrow from each of them to understand our relation to the world. Most people, however, have come to see the futility of making any one of them the center of their faith and trust. This is so because all of them are based on an impersonal view of man. He becomes part of a process, a cog in the ongoing machine of life. The only response to such an understanding of man` is that of resignation or despair.

The World of Men

As a reaction to the impersonal theories of the natural sciences men have tried to explain life in terms of personal and interpersonal relationships. Psychology and sociology have served to make the understanding of man himself the key to a meaningful life.

While biology stresses the animal nature of man, psychology stresses the self-consciousness of man, which separates him from the world of nature. By virtue of his reason man has the capacity to stand above his animal existence and to reflect on it. This is what makes him an individual. He can think and believe and plan and hope. He lives not merely by instinct and natural desire but also by thought and will.

This makes of man a complex being. Since ancient times people have tried to describe his unique nature by using words like body, soul, heart, mind, spirit. Even modern science has not been able to explain satisfactorily the mysterious relationship among a man's instinctive, rational, and emotive qualities.

Under the influence of the scientific method man has been made the object of laboratory investigation. He is examined objectively, much like a machine, to see what makes him tick. Such investigation is valuable but not adequate. It sees man as an individual mechanism within the world of nature, but it fails to see him as a person. Only when the individual is seen in relation to other individuals and groups can he be adequately understood.

Consequently there have developed the sociological studies and theories of the modern era. Man's relationship to his world is seen in terms of his relationship to other human beings, to his place in society, to his culture and tradition. In other words, it is said that man can be understood only when he is seen as a person among persons.

In these studies the scientific approach is used. The emergence of cultures is seen in terms of certain universal laws and the concurrence of accidental forces and events at work in the world. There is an attempt to discover these forces and thereby to predict what may happen under similar circumstances in the future. Sociological, political, and economic theories are developed to help guide men to a fuller understanding of their place in the world.

One serious problem in theories of psychology and sociology is their tendency to relieve a man of individual responsibility. Like the theories of natural science, the social-science theories see man as part of a process, the product of his society and his cultural environment. A crime is committed, and the criminal is excused because it is believed he was the victim of unfortunate circumstances. While most men are ready to acknowledge the relationship between crime and social environment, they are not ready to excuse the criminal by relieving him of all personal responsibility.

It is this conflict between cultural environment and personal responsibility that adds to the perplexing predicament of modern man. The old authorities that spelled out his moral responsibilities have been overthrown. Whereas people in the Western world used to govern their lives by a definite moral code interpreted for them by some authority, today morality is a matter of relative values based on expediency. Most people follow whatever serves their best interests.

So it is that we tend to live for our own material advancement. We live by slogans which reveal our concern for self. "Honesty is the best policy." "It *pays* to be honest." The Golden Rule has been revised to read: "Do good to others so they will do good to you." "One good turn deserves another."

Such a centering of life in self is the inevitable result of understanding our relationship to the world in terms of the world itself. If I am simply a biological accident in an impersonal universe and the product of a culture governed by impersonal laws, I may as well make the most of my opportunities and enjoy as much as possible my few years of life. Whatever serves the purpose of self-enjoyment I shall follow. It's up to *me*.

This is the philosophy of a man who understands his life only in terms of one or more of the above theories regarding the world of nature or the world of men. For him the world of nature is here to serve his own ends. Similarly the world of men centers in himself. Other men are valuable insofar as they serve and satisfy him. He is faithful to his wife as long as she pleases him and no one else pleases him better. He loves another person when it is advantageous to him. He helps another person because of the satisfaction it gives him. He does his job for the personal gain he derives from it. All his relationships with others center in self and are evaluated in terms of his own personal happiness or satisfaction.

This is, in the main, the story of all of us. If we are honest, we see ourselves in this description of a man who understands life on the basis of the world of nature and the world of men. This is why we recognize the need for another dimension to our existence. Our relationship to the world cannot be explained solely by observable facts and their resultant theories. There is something that remains inexplicable about man and his relationship to the world when viewed from a purely scientific basis.

The World of Spirit

Whatever view a man has of the world, he cannot *prove* it true. He simply *believes* it. This is where a new dimension enters his picture of the world — the dimension of the spiritual. Whenever a man centers his life in one or more explanations of his existence, he is doing more than engaging in intellectual observation. He is going beyond the realm of fact into the realm of faith. He is committing himself "spiritually" as well as intellectually. He is revealing the "religious" nature of his being.

There have been many attempts to explain the world

of spirit and its relationship to the world of nature and the world of men. From ancient times it has been believed that spirit exists behind all of what we see and know and that spirit gives life. Among certain ancient peoples it was believed that a whole world of spirits exists behind the visible world. Sometimes these spirits were believed to take on special forms and shapes. They were considered to be divine in nature, emanating from a world spirit called by various names, including the name "god."

Since those days there have been refinements of the idea of spirit. In a less crude way men still try to express that dimension of human existence which goes beyond the observations of reason and science. Popular in the 19th century was the view that the world spirit is revealing itself in everything that happens. Since everything happens logically, there must be a world spirit behind world events.

So it is that the spiritual world is something that man regards as necessary to explain the world he can see and experience. It is this striving for a spiritual understanding of the world and man's relationship to it that is known as "religion." A man is "religious" when he acknowledges spiritual forces operating behind or within the world of experience.

In the Western world religion has often become synonymous with Christianity. Such an identification reveals a misunderstanding of religion. Every man has a religion whether he professes one of the organized forms of religion or not. A man, for example, who believes that pure biology explains his relationship to the world is making the biological process his religion. He is giving to it a spiritual and ultimate dimension. He lives by it; he centers his life in it. In short, the biological process is his god.

The same is true of every man. Whenever anyone makes a statement about the nature of the world and man's relationship to it, he is professing a religion. He is revealing a belief in which he is centering his life. He is giving

14

evidence of belief in a spiritual dimension, in something that goes beyond the scientific observation of the five senses. He is confessing a god whether he admits it or not.

No man can therefore avoid the spiritual and the religious. Every thought about man's relationship to the world has spiritual dimensions and religious implications. Even the philosophers who try to be objectively analytical about the world and man cannot escape the spiritual dimensions of their own personal relationships to the world of nature and the world of men.

Man's problem, then, is not that of having a religion or not having one. It is not a problem of having a god or not having one. It's a matter of recognizing the religion one has and the god one trusts for what they are. It's a matter of knowing what it is that we regard as the center of our being and the goal of our living.

The Three Worlds as One

We live in these three worlds — the world of nature, the world of men, the world of spirit. We have certain ideas about our relationship to these worlds. How do these three worlds converge to make one world — a world that makes sense? How do we come to experience a harmonious relationship to these three worlds? Is there a unifying factor that cuts across all these theories about the world and our relationship to it? In short, is there a single center and a single purpose from which our lives can be oriented?

These are the perplexing questions of human existence. And it seems that the more men know about these worlds, the more perplexed they are. America is more literate than most countries; yet she has more persons with mental and emotional disturbances than they have. We have had many possibilities opened to us, many possible bases to build our lives on, many would-be gods.

This is in the nature of things. Every opportunity,

every blessing given to man is a potential god. Anything that gives him satisfaction may easily become his god. America's gods are many because her people enjoy unprecedented opportunities and possibilities. There are so many "things" making a claim on men's lives, so many potential gods to choose from. The couple whose television set takes precedence over personal responsibilities is attaching spiritual and religious significance to television. The young man who can think of nothing else but his new car and accomplishes little else in life besides washing it and polishing it may be allowing a "thing" to be his god. The teen-age girl who avoids personal responsibilities to spend every waking moment with the latest hit tunes is making a god out of a "thing."

All men have such "things" to which they look for satisfaction and security. They expect these to give meaning to life. But before they know it, these try to take charge. The couple owning a television set may be unaware that the set may very well be owning them. The things over which man has control have a way of controlling him. He invents a bomb to exercise control, but now he finds to his horror that the bomb, not he, is in charge.

It is obvious that the gods which a man allows to control him may become the source of his discouragement and despair. The man who has left his wife because some other woman has greater sex appeal usually finds that his god (or goddess) has let him down. The woman whose life centers in the clothes she wears is never satisfied with what she has, no matter how much or how expensive it may be. The student who lives for popularity is in serious distress when the god of popularity isn't being satisfied.

It is this confusion of gods that causes confusion and perplexity in life. There are so many possible "things" in which to center one's life. The problem is spiritual. It has to do with man's "religious" attitude toward things and people, toward the world of nature and the world of men. He doesn't know which should come first. And when he does give one "thing" precedence, it starts controlling him and then disappointing him because it cannot supply his ultimate needs. This brings a man to ask sooner or later, "Is there any real security in 'things' at all?"

The difficulty lies in trying to find the meaning of life within life itself. Man tries to explain the world of nature on the basis of something within it. He tries to explain the world of men on the basis of something within them. But the world of nature and the world of men can be explained only by something we bring to them. You can explain a rabbit only on the basis of some prior understanding about rabbits. You can explain a machine only on the basis of some prior ideas about machines. You can explain the nature of a friend only on the basis of your prior observations about men in general. Anyone or anything can be explained only on the basis of something that lies outside it.

So it is with the world of nature and the world of men. Taken *as a whole,* the world can be satisfactorily explained only by something or someone that exists prior to it and beyond it. If the relationship between the world of nature, the world of men, and the world of spirit is to be seen in proper perspective, it must be seen by someone who can stand above it (not in terms of space, of course, but in terms of a position beyond or outside it in the same sense that a man can stand outside himself and reflect on himself). If man's relationship to the world is to be understood at all, it must be seen by someone outside of man and beyond the world.

It is the contention of the Christian message that there is such a One. It furthermore contends that this One has revealed Himself. By His revelation He has given the lie to all gods and all religions. Christianity is the end of religions in the sense that it regards all attempts of man to find God as inadequate. Man cannot go beyond the world to find God. Man is finite, confined to the world, not able to reach beyond it.

But God comes to man. It is in His coming, says the Christian, that man experiences a single center of being and a single goal for living. It is by God's coming to us that we are able to understand our relationship to the world.

2

GOD'S CREATION

God comes to us. This is the message of Christianity, and it is this message which distinguishes the Christian religion from religion in general. It says that God breaks into history and reveals Himself to man. He shows Himself to be the Creator and Lord of our existence.

The God of Creation

The Christian's belief in God as Creator is not a mere theory about the origin of the universe. It is a living and personal trust in his Creator. He acknowledges God as the source of all life. He looks beyond the present order of things for meaning and purpose.

But doesn't all religion look for meaning in the beyond, in the world of spirit? It is true that religion in general seeks for something that gives purpose to life. It looks at the world, and on the basis of its observations concludes that there must be a hidden power and purpose behind it all.

On the basis of these observations men construct their ideas about the spiritual dimension behind all things. Some conclude that there is one divine being responsible for the world. Others conclude there are a number of such beings. Regardless of the number, however, the god or gods which men believe in purely on the basis of their own observations are products of their own minds. Man's essentially religious nature causes him to look for divine power beyond himself.

His Relationship to Us. The Christian knows that all these attempts on the part of unbelieving man to discover God end in idolatry. Each society constructs its own idea of God in accord with its own observations and traditions. The result is a number of religions, each with its own set of formulations about divinity and man's relationship to it. All of these attempts are "natural" religions, the results of man's "natural" religious inclination.

The form of natural religion most influential in America is deism, the religion of Thomas Jefferson, Benjamin Franklin, and other men influential in the early years of our nation's history. According to deism, the laws of nature discovered by the emergence of science lead men to acknowledge a supreme being. He is given various names: the Grand Architect, the Great Geometrician, the Master Builder and is often referred to in political speeches and elsewhere as Supreme Being or Almighty God. Yet in their minds this god is hardly more than an impersonal power in the world of nature, whose existence and attributes they deduce by observation and reason — and then worship him.

To this manufactured, impersonal idea of God the Christian Gospel speaks in judgment. It calls the god of deism an idol. Anything that man conceives and constructs and then worships is an idol, something less than God. It is making God conform to man's observations and deductions. The Christian faith contends that God is a "personal" God. This does not mean that He has a "personality" in a psychological sense. We cannot picture Him in terms of our finite and conditioned human form of being a "person." By saying He is personal the Christian believes that God cares about man, takes an interest in him, and reaches out to him. He confesses faith in a God who addresses man in judgment and grace, who comes to him in a "personal" relationship.

This is the way ancient Israel at its best saw God. Her people heard God speak through His prophets and saw His mighty deeds in their history. Theirs was not a god of the mind. He was the God who had offered a special covenant relationship to His people. He revealed to them that He was their God and that He wanted them to be His people.

It is within this covenant relationship that Israel saw its God as Creator of the world. From their experiences of His creating and redeeming activity the Israelites were convinced that it is He who creates and sustains the universe. God brought them to this conviction. The Genesis account of creation is the inspired expression of Israel's belief that God — the God who had revealed Himself to His people — was their Creator and the Creator of all things.

The Christian church has always seen the world in this perspective. It is not primarily concerned about scientific theories regarding the origin of the world and man. Martin Luther reemphasized the Biblical view of creation with its stress on the personal relationship between God and His people. In his explanation of the First Article of the Apostles' Creed Luther began: "I believe that God has created *me* and all creatures." Luther was convinced that no true understanding of the world is possible apart from a personal faith in the God who reveals Himself as *my* Creator. God's creating activity cannot be understood apart from His preserving activity. Only when I trust God as the operating force in my life can I come to confess Him as the Creator and Preserver of the universe. "That He supplies me with all that I need to support this body and life" — this convinces me of His power to create and destroy, to give and withhold. His present relationship to me through faith in the Christ of the Scriptures is the guarantee of His creating and sustaining power.

The Christian Gospel addresses us with a challenge. By giving us a new life in Christ it calls into question all of our natural ideas about God and about the world we live in. We no longer try to understand our place in the world apart from our faith in the God of Scripture. Only out of His "personal" relationship to us and our personal relationship to Him can we understand His relationship and our relationship to the world.

His Relationship to the World of Nature. It is the contention of deism that God operates outside of nature. This view of God's relationship to the world has influenced some Christians and perverted their message. It has frequently caused an unnecessary conflict between science and Christianity. Deism says that the world operates automatically according to natural laws set in motion by God at the beginning. He stands above them like a master technician observing the work of his machine. He is unknowable except through nature and its immutable laws, a supernatural force which operates *reasonably* and *indifferently*.

That this view has influenced Christian tradition is evidenced in attempts to "explain" the miracles of the Bible. Some Christians attempted to meet deism on its own rationalistic grounds. They said: "All right, the world operates by certain immutable laws; but occasionally God steps into the picture and suspends these laws in order to achieve His purpose." But this idea of God "stepping into" the world presupposes that God is not ordinarily present in the world. Only isolated events are His doing; the vast majority of events happen "according to some autonomous laws of nature."

Such a view led to a drastic separation of science and theology. Science went on its way and investigated the world apart from any connection with theological concerns. When it began to discover things that appeared to differ from Biblical concepts of the world, a serious divorce took place, that of Christian theology from scientific investigation. Under these conditions science frequently became a substitute for Christianity. Scientists were considered suspect by the church. Some turned to deism, others to agnosticism, others to a convenient separation of their beliefs as scientists from their beliefs as Christians.

In recent times science and scientists have increasingly become concerned about human values. The discovery of vast resources of power has impressed them with the need for the spiritual fiber necessary to control this power. There is an earnest desire on the part of scientists that the breach between Christianity and science be healed.

Contemporary theology is attempting to speak to this desire. Christianity has the message which addresses itself to the fears of modern man as he enters the nuclear age. It may speak more directly than it often spoke in preceding ages. It is not concerned with mere talk *about* God, but it has a message *from* God. There is a new emphasis in contemporary Christianity on the fact that God *speaks* to men of every century and circumstance. The impersonal god of deistic speculation is being allowed to die, and the living God of heaven and earth is being allowed to speak. The Biblical emphasis on a "personal" God, as taken seriously by Luther, is being allowed to speak to our time through a large number of Christian leaders.

According to this Biblical view, God is seen as directly involved in the affairs of the world. There is no division between God's activity and the world of nature. The world is God's world, the sphere of His activity. The universe also is His domain. He is the God in whom all things have their being. God is not merely "up there" or "out there," but He is "here, there, and everywhere."

Such a realization of God's presence has tremendous implications for living. We have a God who is present in our lives. He does not merely "step into" the world on occasion. His miraculous power is always present. His creative presence can be seen in all the areas of human culture and achievement — in science, medicine, art. There is no area of our existence from which He is absent.

This means we are constantly being challenged by the presence of God. Our birth is more than the result of human copulation. We are here because of God's creative activity. The world is here because of His miraculous, life-giving power. Without Him nothing comes into being. This is the message of Christianity, that the One who is beyond the universe is operative within the universe. Only by faith do we recognize His presence and power in our own lives.

His Relationship to the World of Men. Christian man sees God's rule as operative in the world through His creatures. The Christian view gives to history a different interpretation from the interpretation given it by "religious" man. The ancient Greeks saw history as an endless repetition of events. Their nature gods were a part of this ever-recurring cycle. History was an aimless process in which man was caught. The Israelites, however, saw themselves as people who were led by a concerned God. Life was more than a meaningless succession of events. All their times were in God's hands. He was present in their history — leading, guiding, directing. Every word and deed of God was the means through which God called them to repentance and at the same time offered them a new future. Their repentance and their acceptance of

God's promise was always a new beginning. The past was forgiven them; a new future awaited them.

Similarly the New Testament sees life as a pilgrimage under God to the goal He has set. History is understood in terms of God making all things new by the work of Jesus Christ. History tells of the constant struggle between the kingdom of God and the kingdom of this world.

This means that there is a purpose in history. That God is operative in the world of men means that history is neither an endless cycle of events nor merely a human struggle for meaning and purpose. The eyes of faith in God's redemptive activity enable man to see history as the scene of His judgments and the fulfillment of His promise.

This is the message of Christianity. It says that life is not our own. It says that our times are in God's hands. It says that we stand always under His judgment and His promise. Our place in history can be understood only in the realization of this relationship. Psychological and sociological theories about our place in society are helpful, but apart from the eyes of faith in the goals of God they cannot give ultimate meaning or purpose. Only when we see the world's history and our own history in the light of God's activity within this history can we find our places in this seemingly chaotic and meaningless world.

The God of Order

Every culture in the world is characterized by some sense of order. There are orders of family, society, government, religion. Though the structure of these orders may differ widely from one culture to another, yet the fact remains that a sense of order is built into the nature of man and his society.

These "natural orders" reveal the basically "religious" orientation of man. There is a universal belief in some kind of supreme being. Such a belief is natural to man and reasonable. It is on the basis of such a belief that men have a sense of right and wrong and a conscience. They consider themselves answerable to the god they worship.

From this natural idea of a divine being men recognize certain orders around which their lives are structured. An idea of "family" develops. Patterns of marriage, of tradition, of government begin to emerge. Laws are formulated to stabilize and preserve these patterns. Based on a reasonable approach to what seems good for a given society, such laws determine for its people what is right and what is wrong. These laws are basic for the ordering of the society.

It would seem, according to what is said above, that this ordering of life in the world is accomplished entirely by man apart from God. On the basis of his own idea of a divine being, man formulates his own laws and structures his own society. Yet the Christian believes that none of this takes place apart from God's creative activity. What, then, is the relationship between God and these natural orders?

Christianity contends that natural man does not recognize the true God of order. He may be able to order his life in reasonable fashion, but the true God of order he does not really know. He has become separated from the Source of his being. As the result, most ideas man has about divinity and about God are his own perverted ideas. Every god of natural religion is an idol, conceived in man's mind according to his own pattern.

Similarly, the orders around which man structures his life are not recognized by him for what they are. He sees them as existing apart from God. This is his idea of "natural." Like the Jeffersonian concept of "natural" rights, man sees his idea of order and law as an inherent part of his "natural" constitution. This is the surest sign of man's apartness from God — his pitting of the natural against the divine. By such a distinction he is saying that part of his life is governed by natural causes and the rest by divine motivations.

For the Christian of the Protestant tradition such a distinction is misleading. There is no "natural" realm *apart* from God. Every order of society is under Him, and every so-called natural order exists by His ordination and permission. For this reason we prefer to speak of the orders *of creation* rather than the *natural* orders, since the word "natural" has come to be placed vis-à-vis the divine.

Your Station in Life. Luther spoke of the orders of creation as the "secular" realm. This does not mean that he separated them from the creating activity of God. His distinction between the secular and spiritual realms served the purpose of explaining the orientation of the Christian in this world. He showed thereby what Christians have in common with all men and also what distinguishes them from society in general.

Every man is a part of the secular realm. As part of a family, of a society, of a government every man has a position in life. He is either father or mother, son or daughter, employer or employee, ruler or subject. Also the church in its institutional aspect is a secular order with stations and ranks.

Now, all of these orders and stations of the secular realm are divinely ordained. They are "natural" only in the sense that they operate for all men, also for those who live apart from God. They are accepted by unconverted man as well as the Christian, both by men who do not recognize them as divine orders and by those who do.

Furthermore, the secular orders might be called "natural" orders because they are fallen orders. In the New Testament "natural man" means fallen man — man in his apartness from God. Similarly the secular orders are natural in the sense that they represent orders corrupted by man's sin. In themselves they are not sinful, but they are used for sinful ends because of the sinfulness of man.

As human beings we participate in the orders of creation. As sinful human beings we have corrupted these orders. But Christians see these orders in a new way through the redemption by Christ. They recognize that these orders in themselves are not sinful but perfect in their givenness by God. Because God has made us a part of His spiritual realm in Christ, we see our position in life as part of a divine calling. A person becomes a parent not merely by natural choice or chance but by the call of God. Our occupying certain positions in life is not the result of our effort or of fate or of accidence; we were called by God.

For us as Christians every secular position becomes a spiritual calling because we recognize in everything the creating activity of the God who comes to us in judgment and mercy. His Law is constantly judging us in our particular areas of service. By the same token His Word of forgiveness in Christ is constantly justifying us and enabling us to carry out our respective callings faithfully and effectively by being loving parents, obedient children, faithful employers or employees, loyal rulers or subjects, true servants of God and men.

Our Bondage and Freedom. The Christian's place in the world is seriously affected by the sin which clings to him. Life for him is a constant struggle between his carnal desires and his spiritual motivations. Every position in life is attended by demonic temptations. The "natural" orders tend to replace God and to enslave man by their demands.

This bondage of the "natural orders" can be illustrated in various ways. The order of marriage becomes a source of bondage because of the pride and selfishness of its participants. The orders of family and society become a source of demonic oppression because of the self-centeredness of men. The order of government may become a living hell because of the arrogance and vanity of men.

To a greater or lesser degree all men know the bondage of the secular orders. In every case it is the sinfulness of man which is responsible. The apartness from God which characterizes natural man enslaves him through the created orders to a life of insecurity and fear. This is the bondage of our creaturely existence.

In fact, the very existence of natural orders is all the more necessary because of man's sin. The government, for example, exists for the purpose of keeping order in the world. It punishes the evildoer. Were it not for human sin, the power of the sword would not be necessary. Similarly laws concerning the order of marriage would be unnecessary but for man's perverted nature.

But more than this, sin affects the very understanding and expression of the natural orders. When men try to formulate laws to govern the orders of society, they do so on the basis of reason. Since man's understanding is also corrupted by his self-centeredness and bondage, the very formulations of the principles which are to govern him may be expressions of sinful desires. An exaggerated example is the "reasonable" setting up of a superstate based on "reasonable" ideas of a superrace as proposed by Nazism. Similarly, certain "reasonable" formulations concerning marriage customs reveal the perversion resulting from man's apartness from God.

Every perversion, then, of the natural orders results from man's bondage to the old Adam and to the ideas he has about life. Even the laws he makes might enslave him and take away his freedom. In place of serving God, he serves law. In so doing he makes the law his god. He loses the freedom of a direct relationship to the Source of his being.

It is the message of Christianity that this freedom has been restored for man. It comes to him as a gift. It is bestowed through God's revelation of Himself in the person of Jesus Christ. This will be more fully described in the next chapter. Suffice it to say here that there is the possibility of freedom in this creaturely existence when a man by God's grace is drawn into a saving and sanctifying relationship with God. In this relationship a man is rescued from the control of the alien powers which pervert the orders of creation.

Such freedom is not what man naturally conceives freedom to be. His idea of freedom is also corrupted because he sees freedom as originating in himself. He thinks there is freedom apart from God, the freedom to do as he pleases according to his carnal inclinations. But such freedom is always slavery. Man is enslaved to his ideas of freedom. When he begins to exercise such "freedom," he soon comes to the rude awakening that it is slavery. The things he thought he was free to follow enslave him, and he finds himself serving them. He may try another course, but he finds that this, too, enslaves him.

There is no "natural" freedom, then, which is not actually bondage. But there is a "bondage" which actually is freedom. It is the bondage to Christ, who by His redemptive life and death has earned for men freedom from sin and Satan. This is the message of Christianity. When a man is bound to the Source of his being, he is free. When God calls a man to a relationship of obedience to Himself, such a man is truly free. Man's obedience to the Creator of all orders of life reveals to him a new dimension. The secular becomes sacred, the sinful becomes transformed, the humdrum becomes meaningful. This is what happens when faith in God meets the facts of life.

Our Responsibility. Faith in God's offer of forgiveness and sonship through Christ realizes itself in responsible attitude and activity within the orders of creation. The Christian sees all of life as the realm of God's activity and himself as the agent of God's intention for men. He views the orders of creation as the means for serving his fellowmen, all of whom are God's creatures whether they recognize it or not.

The Christian recognizes his responsibility to help men realize their creatureliness and to acknowledge their Creator. He wants them to share the freedom of forgiveness, to be raised above slavery and to experience relationship with the Creator Himself.

Such a relationship with the Creator cannot be possible without His message of redemption. Men cannot know God as Creator unless they know Him as Redeemer. And His redemption cannot be known apart from God's revelation in Jesus Christ. Christians recognize the God of creation and life in the person of Jesus of Nazareth. In Him all of God's purposes are revealed.

There have been many attempts to find a relationship with God apart from the redemption offered in Christ. They can be summed up under three main types: mysticism, legalism, rationalism. Mysticism tries to achieve union with God by ecstatic experience, by an effort to allow oneself to "melt" into the divine, by "feeling" some kind of spiritual contact with God. Legalism represents the efforts of man to reach God by following laws and principles which he regards as expressions of God's will. Rationalism believes that man's reason is the expression of the divine in him and that God can therefore be reached by the exertion of the mind.

It can readily be seen that all of these attempts to reach God begin with man. Apart from God's revelation of Himself, they are presumptuous efforts to determine what God is like and when and how He relates to men. God becomes what man sees Him to be and thereby is reduced to an idol, the product of man's intuition or will or reason.

To every such "religious" view of God the Scripture speaks in judgment and says: "Man does not come to God, but God comes to man." How do we know this is true?

31

We see it in Jesus Christ. In Him God came to sinful men who did not seek Him. In Him God came to redeem all men for His service in the orders of creation. This is the Word from God to which Christians witness as they live in the orders of creation. This Word opens up every position in life as a Christian vocation. As Christians we now see all of life as part of God's creative activity. We see our place in the world in terms of responsibility to Him and to all our fellow creatures under Him.

The God of Law

The "orders of creation" are orders of law. Natural man, despite his apartness from God, retains a sense of law. This law is frequently referred to as "natural law." It should be kept in mind that knowledge of this law has been perverted by sin, even as have the natural orders. Therefore the "law in the heart" of which Paul speaks in the New Testament is insufficient.

Yet this "natural law" is of divine origin. As such it serves as the basis for the ordering of society. It finds expression in various forms and in every culture. Luther saw in the Ten Commandments the expression of the kernel of "natural law." It is the expression of God's divine Law for His people. The Israelites recognized this Law as divine. They knew themselves to be in a covenant relationship with God. For them the Ten Commandments were not the words of men but of God.

The Law of Israel served God's purpose. It kept order in their society, and it judged them as individuals and as a nation. This is the function of law. Whether written or unwritten, the Law serves this twofold purpose. Without it the orders of society could not exist. There would be chaos as each man became a law to himself. It is by a consensus of "rightness" and "wrongness," by its comprehension of law, that a given society structures its life. In spite of corrupt interpretations and applications of the Law, God's creative activity is operative through it.

The second function of the Law of God is not as universally recognized. Man does not like to be called to account. He does not see the law as the judging and condemning voice of God. American democracy often prefers to think of the law as the emanation of something good within man himself. It thinks of law in terms of promise. It says that the inherent "rightness" in man will win out if given the opportunity.

Many things have happened in the past several decades to destroy this misguided optimism. Although the old ideas persist, especially in political speeches, there is a sense of judgment on the part of modern man. God has spoken through the events of recent years. He is speaking words of judgment over our self-infatuation. The wars, the pressures of our economic life, the corruption of men in high places, the assassination of President Kennedy — all of these have led man to a greater openness to hear words of judgment.

It is necessary, however, that these words of judgment are heard as the Word of God. Anything less will simply throw man back on his own efforts to improve the situation. It is only when we as individuals and as a nation hear the judgment of *God* upon us and our society that there is any hope for the future. Only then can we receive from Him the remedy for our dilemma.

The failure to see the judging character of God's Law is coupled with the false distinction between so-called natural law and divine Law. Ever since the rise of the natural sciences men have understood the universe in terms of laws. Because the church frequently discouraged the discovery of these laws, they came to be viewed as being apart from Christian theology and even in opposition to it. The law of gravity and other laws of the physical sciences came to be known as natural laws. Frequently they were not seen as part of the creating activity of God.

Christian theologians sometimes mistakenly encouraged this separation by their aloofness from the natural sciences. When they did try to come to terms with these, they capitulated the dynamic view of creation as an ongoing process and allowed the natural sciences to exist separately. Accordingly, scientists frequently did not understand themselves to be subject to the judging and renewing Word of God.

In this context most of Christendom came to develop a static view of creation. The creating activity of God was confined to His "work" at the beginning, to the original creation. What happened since then was seen only as His *preserving* activity. By this was meant that God established the laws of nature at the beginning and that now they operate almost wholly by themselves, except on occasions when He "steps in" to "suspend" them. Creation was considered to be God's once-for-all activity at the beginning of things, not His ongoing activity in the structure of the world and the affairs of men.

Such a static view of creation opened the doors to a divorce of theology from what came to be called the natural sciences. Physics, biology, psychology, sociology developed apart from the judging and sanctifying activity of God. The world and the affairs of men came to be understood in terms of "natural" causes. God became the "Big Boss" upstairs, who is only indirectly concerned with the world He once created, the Master Architect, who turned over the world's operation to impersonal laws which merely need to be "discovered."

Now, it is true that the world operates according to certain basic laws. This does not mean that man makes these laws real by discovering them. He is merely describing something which takes place in the universe whether man realizes it or not. The law of gravity is not a human invention. People fell out of windows before anyone knew about the law of gravity. All the so-called laws of natural science are merely the descriptions of the constant phenomena operative in God's world.

But the Christian does not see these laws apart from the creative hand of God. Every instance of a child falling to the ground, not upward into the sky, is evidence of the activity of the Creator and His way of ruling the universe. There is nothing that happens apart from His creative and sustaining power.

It is this sense of the presence of God *in the world* that frequently has been missing in Christian thinking for centuries. God has been relegated to a position conveniently apart from His world. Man has been operating under the assumption that he is in charge of this planet. Oh, yes, God is in the sky ready to offer His occasional help when *man* asks for it. But otherwise the world is what *he* makes of it.

This view of God's relationship to His world has influenced our Western view of morals and ethics. We have come to develop moral theories centering in ourselves, apart from the Word of God. Systems of ethics based on reason or intuition tell us that man has a basic "sense of ought" which reason or conscience can discover. Aesthetic and existentialist ethics say that the only meaning to life is what we give to it *now* in our own attempts to give life beauty and dignity. Pragmatic ethics says that life should be ordered around what is *useful* for the individual or the greatest number of people. Man and society are the measure of what is right and wrong.

Most Americans live by a combination of these ethical theories. In our apartness from God, as natural men, we live according to the pattern which best serves our selfish natures. Apart from the judging God, all of these theories serve our natural inclinations most admirably. Every theory of ethics apart from relationship to the Creator is

35

the product of what men call the natural law. The proponent of each of these theories believes that life according to his theory is the natural way for man to live out his existence.

But men forget that their ideas of what is natural have been perverted by an "unnatural" alienation from God. The Creator made us for communion with Himself, in His own image. We have destroyed that image, that relationship with Him which He intended as the natural relationship. In our apartness from Him we and the whole world have longings and desires which are unnatural. What we consider natural, therefore, may be actually unnatural in the sight of God. Men can realize their true natures only when they are reunited with the Creator of their natures.

Before this reconciliation with the Creator can take place, there must be a recognition of man's alienation. It is to this alienation that the Law of God speaks. It judges us and scrutinizes both our ethical systems and our scientific theories. It challenges any human system which purports to offer man salvation on the basis of a natural understanding of the world. It shatters any hope that man has of being the captain of his own salvation and the master of his own soul.

This judgment does not minimize the importance of the natural and behavioral sciences for an intelligent understanding of the world and its people. It demands, however, that all of man's knowledge and activity conforms at all times to God's standards. It demands that men come to acknowledge that there is no natural law of science or morality apart from Him. It demands that we see all of our own attempts to formulate laws and codes as the attempts of sinful men and that behind them stands the divine moral order which alone is truly natural, which alone corresponds to the nature of the world as He created it.

The failure to see God's Law in its function of judgment has consistently led the world of men to misuse the Law. In Biblical times the Mosaic Law came to be used as a means of winning favor with God. The Law became the way to God. To the extent that this happened, Judaism became a false religion, and the Jews ceased to be the covenant people of God. Similarly people have always been tempted to make of Christ a new lawgiver and to regard His Sermon on the Mount as a means for reaching up to God. This is characteristic of fallen man's "religious" nature, that he proposes to attain divine favor according to his own ideas of right and wrong before God and by his own works.

Such religious systems within Christendom have developed in the area not only of Christian conduct but also of Christian doctrine. The intellectual acceptance of certain formulations of belief often became the sole criterion of man's relationship to God. Such an emphasis is just as arrogantly "religious" and man-determined as one which grants salvation on the basis of a code of conduct.

Christians, too, need desperately to hear the Law of God. By this time it should be clear that the Law of God refers not merely to the written formulations of man's comprehension of His Law. To hear God's Law means to hear His Word of judgment on every area of our human existence. Most certainly His voice is heard through the written record of His Law. Christians believe that in the Holy Scriptures God speaks authoritatively to man's predicament and judges his sin. The Bible reveals to man his separation from God, his unnatural existence apart from the Creator. Here God speaks in judgment on every thought and word and deed of all men of all times.

All of us stand under this accusing finger of God. So does our nation. So does every aspect of our culture. Any evaluation of our lives and of our country ought to consist not merely in an examination of "natural" causes. It must hear the accusing and condemning voice of God as

He speaks in His Word. Our hope and that of America does not lie in morbid outcries and lamentations about the existing situation. It lies not in our trying to reach God by surface sorrow or pragmatic repentance. It lies rather in God, in His cutting and condemning Word of judgment, and in His bringing us to genuine repentance and to genuine recognition of our unnatural existence apart from Him.

Our Creator speaks to us — in judgment. His Law tells us that we are not truly human apart from Him. Only through reconciliation with Him can we become the human beings He created us to be. Only the Creator can accomplish our rescue, and it is His desire to do so. He says so. And all He asks is that we acknowledge our creatureliness, our helplessness before His anger, our guilt before His judgment. To such a confession He leads us in order that He might bring us to saving faith in the redemptive life and death of Jesus Christ.

GOD'S REDEMPTION

God's Son has redeemed mankind, has paid the full price for forgiveness, life, and salvation for all men of all time. This is the Word of promise which accompanies God's Word of judgment. God cuts in order to heal. The knife of His Law is always accompanied by the healing power of His Gospel.

Christians recognize this twofold character of God's Word throughout the Scriptures. They hear God addressing them all through the Bible in terms of Law and Gospel, judgment and grace. The Law, as the previous chapter endeavored to show, judges and condemns man and all that is sinful in the institutions of his society and culture. The Gospel offers man forgiveness and help through the work of Christ. It proclaims the good news that Christ has reconciled all things to God, even the world corrupted by man's sin.

The Law of God is understood properly only when it is seen as serving the Gospel. Its function is preparatory. According to Luther, the Law is the means God uses to rule all men in His kingdom of the left hand, the state, while the Gospel is His means to rule only believers in His kingdom of the right hand, the church. The Law is that Word of God which keeps order in the world. Even corrupt or inadequate governments serve people under God's Law. But the Law also prepares men for God's justifying activity. It reveals man's inability to enter into communion with his Creator without the power of the Spirit through the Gospel. It condemns all efforts of man to replace the Creator with creaturely systems and institutions.

To man under condemnation of the Law God speaks in the Gospel, His Word of love, redemption, forgiveness. The Spirit of God by means of the Gospel converts and renews man and enables him to realize his place in the world.

The God of Redemption

Christians contend that God's redeeming activity has been fully revealed in the person and work of Jesus Christ. In Him all the promises of God are fulfilled. He is the Word made flesh, the incarnation of the God of heaven and earth, the manifestation of His power and love.

Such an acknowledgement cannot be proved. Christians do not presume to be able to demonstrate on purely rational and historical grounds their faith in Jesus Christ as the revelation of God. They are convinced that His kingdom does not come with observation but that it comes as a hidden gift from the Creator Himself. Faith in Jesus Christ is the "given" from which the Christian proceeds to order his life. Without this "given" all that he says appears as nonsense to the skeptic and the "nonbeliever." The

Christian understands his place in the world only from this perspective of faith. He makes the claim that Christ redeemed his total being — his reason, his will, his emotions, everything about him. It is only by this faith that he understands his place in the world.

The gospels of the New Testament describe the life and death of Jesus of Nazareth. Through the eyes of faith they see the events from the birth of Bethlehem to the victory of Easter as the manifestation of God's redeeming activity. The gospels emphasize that the kingdom of God has entered the world of man in Jesus Christ. God is present among men.

Christians see in the incarnation and work of Christ the answer to man's attempts to work out his own system of living. The birth of Bethlehem brings hope because it reveals the downward movement of the relationship between God and man. It shows that the Creator of heaven and earth does not leave His rebellious creatures to themselves. He comes to man.

This coming is not a fake performance. God did not merely appear *like* a man. He took on our humanity. Luther loved to speak of *God* wrapped in the swaddling clothes of Bethlehem's manger. This is the miracle of Christmas, that God becomes man and dwells among men.

The presence of God was revealed in Christ throughout His life. Every word and every deed were manifestations of the presence of God to those who had the eyes to see and the ears to hear. His parables were revelations of the nature of God's kingdom. His miracles were demonstrations of God's presence among men. His words were the expressions of God's judgment and the promises of His grace.

The highest expression of God's sharing of our humanity took place at Calvary. Christ's perfect obedience, even unto death, was the ultimate revelation of God's redemptive love for men. All the temptations and burdens Jesus

41

had shared now find their climax in the cross as He in love gives His very life for all men. The cross has been the center of Christian preaching because it is the climactic completion of Christ's work to redeem the world. All the sinfulness of man was revealed for what it is, while the loving concern of God was revealed for what it is. Law and Gospel, sin and grace, judgment and redemption stand out in bold relief as God's Son agonizes and dies in humble submission to His heavenly Father.

This scene of death is for Christians the source of life. It introduces the message that Christ has overcome death by His victorious resurrection. Easter assures us that the living God is present among men. In the midst of death we are in life. "Whether we live or die, we are the Lord's." God is present with His people at all times. The ascension underscores this assurance. The risen and ascended Christ is forever present among men as the assurance of God's life and power. By the sending of His Spirit we are assured at all times that God has not left us to ourselves but that we are His people.

A similar faith characterized the Old Testament people of God. Through their patriarchs and prophets the Israelites heard the voice of God. Through their history they saw the activity of God. They had a real sense, in their better days, of the presence of God. Faith in God's promises enabled them to expect the redemption of God. It constantly opened up to them a new future. The judgment spoken by the prophets was always accompanied by the promise of deliverance.

The Christian sees the anticipation of ancient Israel for deliverance fully realized in Jesus Christ. His kingdom is different from what many in Israel had come to expect. But it is God's kingdom, the kingdom which cannot be compared with the kingdoms of this world. It is not a kingdom of law; it is the kingdom of grace. It does not dictate; it draws. It does not compel; it simply comes to those who receive it.

This kingdom of God in Christ is received by *faith*. When the Christian speaks of faith, he is talking about something that does not originate in himself but comes as a gift from God. Faith in Christ is God's gift of Himself as expressed in the Christian. Faith in Christ is God enabling a person to receive His forgiving love as revealed in Jesus Christ. Certainly the individual participates in the act of faith, but his ability to do so is the work of God, of the power of His Holy Spirit.

Such faith is not merely a belief in facts about Christ. Faith is confidence that God is gracious and forgiving through the living Christ. The man of faith says: "God is gracious. The gracious God is at hand. I can do all things through Christ. Whether I live or die, I am the Lord's."

It is out of this faith in Christ that the believer humbly, reverently, fearfully speaks about Christ. The theology of the church grows out of a man's commitment to Christ. He cannot but speak the things which he has seen and heard. Although he realizes his limitations, the believer wants to talk about his relationship to Christ. He knows that all language is insufficient for his purpose. Nothing can describe adequately the mysterious grandeur of God's presence among men. But he tries. His faith relationship must express itself in words which are his Christian theology and in deeds which are his Christian life.

So it was with the writers of the New Testament. Filled with the Spirit of God they wrote what they had seen and heard. Through them God speaks, so that men might believe on Him and have life. The Scriptures are the Word of life. The church recognizes them as such. They are the only authoritative Word of God to men. They are the means of grace through which God draws men to faith in Himself and in the promise of His presence and power.

We are challenged by the Christian Scriptures to hear

God's offer of redemption. To hear Scripture is to hear God Himself. There is no other message that speaks authoritatively. There are, of course, people who think they hear God speaking to them apart from Scripture. Faith in any such alleged immediate revelation is a delusive misadventure. The god of the golf course or the god of the great outdoors is the kind of god that the man who believes in him *wants* him to be. He is the product of a man's imagination, not the God who addresses him in judgment and grace. The God of the Bible and of Christian preaching is the God who addresses us where we are, not where we think ourselves to be. He sees down into the depths of our being and judges what stands between us and Him. Then He follows this judgment by speaking to the specific obstacle that keeps us from Him. He offers and gives us the grace of Christ, the power of His kingdom, and the faith that saves.

God offers us His redemption in Christ through the message of the Bible. Those who receive it can testify to its power. They can't prove its truth to others in the way that someone can prove the law of gravity. They simply say to men that it's true, that it brings power and peace, love and life. They believe it's the only reliable Word in this confused world of many words. They say that only this Word is God's Word to men, the Word of life.

The God of Life

It is in Jesus Christ that God is revealed as the Creator and Preserver of the world. Apart from Him the God of creation cannot be known. Apart from God's coming in Christ man is left to his own "religiosity." He observes the world and tries to deduce a god or gods on the basis of his observations. But this god is always less than the Creator. It is always a god of one's own mind or a god of fancy. It is always man's idea about deity. It is a religion, but a false religion; it worships something less than God.

The incarnation of God in Christ is not man's idea. It is God's invasion of our lives. It reveals God to us. This does not mean that God is not present at all times in His world. He is, but our sin prevents us from recognizing His presence. Our apartness from Him, our natural blindness, keeps us from seeing God for what He is.

In Christ that presence of God is revealed. God is recognized in Jesus of Nazareth. God became incarnate to redeem the world He had created and to call man from his sin of thinking he is the master of his own destiny. By participating in creation, by taking on our creatureliness, God revealed once and for all His living presence among men — clearly and unmistakably.

Christ and Creation. Christ's coming reveals the goodness of God's creation. "The Word became flesh." God took on our humanity. There were religions in the days of Christ's appearing which regarded the flesh, in the sense of man's body, as sinful. They thought of the body as an evil place of residence for the soul, necessary excess baggage which the soul must endure and struggle against.

The incarnation of God in Christ gives the lie to such a false notion. Christ appeared in a human body and by this act showed the goodness of God's creation. He showed that the flesh as such is not sinful but the precious gift of a loving Creator. He gave man a new and deep appreciation of the goodness of his bodily existence as God intended it and created it.

On the other hand, God became incarnate to redeem men who used the body as *occasion* for sin. Because of man's separation from the Creator, he uses his precious body for vile and selfish purposes. Since man is a fallen being, his body is a source of temptation and a constant threat to his existence. Its sensitivity and its corruptibility are always leading man to frustration and fear. This is due, however, not to any evil in the body itself but to the fallen state of man as a whole.

45

This leads us to a second feature about man's creation which Christ's incarnation emphasizes: the unity of a man's being. In His whole ministry Christ revealed God's concern for man's total being. The incarnate Christ brings the power of God to men and offers them a saving and healing relationship to their Creator. By His own assertion to the disciples of John, the kingdom of God could be seen through His healing of the sick, the lame, the blind. These evidences of God's presence among men assure us that He is concerned for man in his totality, that the God who is seen in Christ is indeed the Creator of their lives.

This concern of Christ for the whole man is the concern that man *as a person* is brought into relationship with God. He did not conceive it to be his mission to save a man's soul apart from his body. He came to save man as such. By announcing God's forgiveness He offers to restore men to their true relationship with their Creator. Through the assurance of this new relationship those who receive the Kingdom experience the power and gracious presence of their Creator Himself.

It was because of Christ's oneness with the Creator that He could authoritatively speak His forgiveness and at the same time reveal His creative power in word and deed. As He said to the paralytic, the one was as easy for Him as the other. It was as easy for Him to say, "Arise, take up your bed and walk," as to say, "Your sins are forgiven you." He who redeemed man is the same God who created him. His redemption in Christ reveals His creation and His preservation of all things, particularly of man.

So it is that the redeeming God in Christ speaks to us where we are. His word of forgiveness speaks to our situation in life. It does not tell us to escape from the realities of our present existence. It does not tell us to withdraw from the world. It reveals the forgiving power at hand in and for the world. It assures us that the Kingdom is present here and now. This is the message of God's redemption, that God, who has overcome all evil powers by the death and resurrection of Christ, breaks into our human situation and establishes His rule over us. In Christ heaven breaks in upon earth, and those who receive it are assured of the victorious power of God. Even though that power is only imperfectly experienced because of our persistent rebellion, we know that its perfect realization awaits us. That future glory is present now in Christ, but it remains for us to experience it perfectly at the final consummation.

Christ is a Participant in our creaturely existence, but He is also the Lord of creation. Easter revealed that creation cannot contain its Creator. The Lord of life revealed His power over the creaturely existence He had taken upon Himself. Here is the complete assurance that our Redeemer is also our Creator, the Lord of life.

The ascension of Christ, all but forgotten in American Christendom, is the crowning revelation of the fact that the risen Christ fills all things with His presence. There is no part of creation which is not glorified by His redemption. For those who receive Him the whole universe is the scene of His activity. No part of His creation is base or common. It is His world, and He is King of kings and Lord of lords.

Because of his relationship to the Creator and Lord of the universe, the Christian sees the created world as a sign of the Creator. God is present in the laboratory and in the forest. He is not the "religious" god of nature, the product of man's imagination. He is the God who has revealed Himself in Jesus Christ. Since the Christian lives in relationship with Him, he is enabled to acknowledge His creation.

This has great significance for the Christian's life. His whole participation in life becomes a response to his Creator and Lord. He sees his task as holy and good. He knows the source of his wisdom and strength. He approaches his responsibilities in life with the assurance of the presence of the God of life. He uses the creation of God in loving response and willing service.

Christ and the Law. In leading man to faith in the redemption of Christ, the Spirit of God raises man above the orders of creation to direct relationship with God. The laws which govern those orders no longer hold man prisoner, but they serve his new status as a child of God.

Like everyone else, the Christian is subject to the laws of society. We saw in the previous chapter that these laws are in themselves good insofar as they are expressions of God's Law. Moreover, they are the means through which God reveals to men their sinfulness and alienation from Him.

While the laws of men may be good, they are also the occasion for evil. What was said regarding man's body applies to God's gift of Law. Because of man's perversion, he uses the Law for his own misguided ends. The Law enslaves when man regards it as the source of life, when he allows the laws of creation to supplant the Creator. This is the pride of fallen man, to think that he can reach the Creator by keeping the laws of the created orders of society. This is man's folly. This is the obstacle that stands in the way of God's coming to him. He refuses to allow God to come, because he insists on taking the initiative himself. His "religious" inclination prevents him from hearing God. He is held captive by the Law, and the more he struggles, the tighter its grip. The more he seems to succeed in keeping it, the greater his pride. Every act supposedly in keeping with the Law brings forth another shout of triumph: "Look, God, see what I've done!"

Such enslavement makes life a hopeless striving. It can lead a man to a high standard of outward morality and achievement. But it also leads him either to self-righteousness or to despair. Either a man becomes self-complacent over his success in doing what he considers right and good, or he despairs at his inability to do what he senses he should be doing. In either case the Law is leading away from the life that God gives.

Into this predicament of man under the Law Christ came. He revealed the basic goodness of the Law by subjecting Himself to it. At the same time He revealed that obedience to the Law need not mean the relinquishing of a man's freedom. He showed that man is not made for the Law, but the Law for man. By His own life and death he revealed the divine power which enables a man to keep the Law willingly. His oneness with God enabled Him to judge the laws of men in terms of their service to man. His keeping of the Law was done out of the realization of its divine origin. He saw the Law as the gift of a loving God, not as the burden of a tyrant. God was not for Him the heavenly policeman who rules by force. He revealed that the Law, as operative in God's kingdom of the left hand, receives its true significance through the Gospel, as operative in the kingdom of God's right hand.

Christ's subjection to the Law proved therefore to be "the end of the Law." This does not mean that the Law of God is abolished. It means rather that it is fulfilled. Therefore in his renewed relationship with God the Christian no longer looks to the Law for motivation. He finds it in the Gospel, the good news of his redemption by Christ, which the Holy Spirit uses as the means to fill him with grateful love and devotion. This is the only truly enabling power there is. It is not a power which forces itself on a man, does not compel the good, but seeps into a man's inner being and initiates an inner compulsion to live in response to God.

For the Christian the Law is changed from master to servant. The Law is a divine gift and guide, showing him how he can live out his faith relationship as a child of his Creator and a participant in the Creator's world. By faith in Christ he receives the freedom to choose to do the good.

He is "out from under" the Law's demands and uses the Law to live freely the life of a redeemed creature whose reason and will are motivated by the mind of the Christ who lives within him. This is the end of the Law and the beginning of life, the life which God intends for man.

Christ and the Person. The non-Christian life under the Law is associated in the New Testament with death. Apart from Christ, you are dead. To be sure, non-Christians *exist* on this planet. But they do not "live." Authentic life is possible only when there is a living relationship with the Lord of life. Apart from this relationship, what seems like life is really a living death, separation from God. This is an existence apart from the Source of life. It is existence under the Law. It is a "religious" existence in which man pretends to know the source and end of his being but always remains apart from it. He develops a philosophy of what he regards to be life, but he knows it will end. He can't escape the fact of his deathbound existence.

Death stares all of us in the face. It cannot be avoided. The Christian message says to us, however, that in the midst of death we are in life. For the one who has accepted the call by the Creator of life into His kingdom there is no death. What appears to be death is the full realization of life.

This assurance shapes the Christian's whole present perspective. Sickness, suffering, temptation, discouragement — all of these cannot contain man, for he knows the life which lies behind and beyond his creaturely existence. He is committed to that life and to its Creator. Nothing can keep it from coming through, not even death. It is the life which persists because it is life from God.

This is the life which Christ has revealed to us. This is the life He came to give back to man, the life that God intended every man to have but which in Adam all men lost. In Christ that life is restored. He is the second Man, the man of God, the God-man. He is what humanity was intended to be.

This Man wants to give to men their true humanity. He wants to make whole persons out of us. He is the Healer. In German the word for Savior is *Heiland*, the one who heals. This is appropriate. He heals men from the sickness of separation from God. He turns death into life.

That perfect wholeness which Christ came to bring will not be perfectly realized until the final denouement. Then all that keeps tearing our lives apart will be done away. Our relationship with God will be unhindered and unencumbered by the death which still clings to us. Then all that smacks of death and separation will be absent. There will be no sin and therefore no suffering and sorrow but only joy and peace.

This prospect of what is to come is our assurance in the present. This heaven is continually breaking into our present existence, trying to speak to us and raise us up above our old earthbound ambitions. As pilgrims we journey toward the day, daily drowning the old Adam of death and trusting the Lord of life to keep us in the true faith by the comfort and power of His grace and love.

The God of Love

In the Christian's encounter with Jesus Christ he sees the God of his creation and redemption as the God of love. The life of Christ and His death reveal the underlying principle of love with which God carries on His creating and regenerating activity in this world.

There have been numerous attempts in past years to define the love of God and to distinguish it from the forms of human love. In many cases these attempts have led to a questionable divorce of natural love from divine love.

The words which express this distinction are *eros* and *agape*. The former is often seen as natural in the sense that it originates within the created world, and the latter is regarded as the love which comes from God. Now this may be a valuable distinction, but it should not be pressed to the point where *eros* is something evil and only *agape* is divine. This is an oversimplification. Even as all Law is of divine origin, so all love is of God. To be sure, the love with which God created the world is not seen for what it is because of the perversion of man. Even as he attempts to find the way to God, so man struggles to determine the character of love. Man's *eros* is his attempt to love.

This attempt by men to understand the nature of love is thwarted by his fallen character. It is "erotic" not in the popular sense of the word but in the sense that it reflects man's separation from God. It always comes short of the love which is from God. While this attempt of man's "religious" nature to discover the love that operates in the universe is imperfect, it should be stressed that *eros* is not in itself evil. *Eros* is a part of man's nature, which God uses in governing the world of men. It has led to a high expression of moral values and law. It has led to fine examples of heroic and unselfish service to fellowmen.

The marriage union is regulated by higher or lower expressions of *eros*. Similarly societies and states are governed by expressions of *eros,* and it is this *eros* which makes the world a reasonably fit place to live. *Eros* is responsible for the many expressions in literature and art of the beauty of God's creation. Man's *eros* serves a necessary and useful purpose in the world.

And yet *eros* is the "human" way of loving, and since every man is a part of fallen mankind, his *eros* is to a lesser or greater degree always propelled by his selfish ambitions and desires. It loves and serves what it finds lovable and self-satisfying. Now, it is not wrong to be attracted to some people more than others. The New Testament appears to give evidence that Christ was attracted to John, no doubt finding particular satisfaction in John's company. But this attraction was accompanied by something more. When an individual engages in the highest form of love, he goes beyond the love produced by attraction. He is concerned not with satisfying self but with satisfying the object of his love. Higher love is more concerned with giving than receiving. Higher love forgives the imperfections in what it loves. Higher love loves also when its object is unlovable.

It is this kind of unselfish, self-emptying love that the Scriptures call *agape*. This is the love that characterizes God. His is the love that simply flows out. It loves regardless of the unlovableness of what it loves. This is not just an *attitude* in God. It is the very nature and essence of God. "God is Love." That love of God is revealed conclusively in the mission and work of Jesus Christ. In spite of man's alienation and rebellion God reveals His love in the self-sacrificing life and death of His Son. Christ is the human incarnation of *agape*, of the God of love.

This love, as revealed in Christ, transforms our present relationships. "We love because He first loved us." By faith in Christ as the Revelation of perfect *agape*, we children of God are enabled to love unselfishly. *Agape* permeates our human relationships. It purifies *eros* and completes it. While we may be drawn by something in another person, we now see that God Himself is present in this relationship. We are propelled by His love to see others as objects of that same love. The Christian receives the power from God to live "in tune" with this perfect love to serve as its agent and channel. His *eros*, his feeble attempt to know love apart from Christ, is now transformed by *agape*, by the love that comes from God.

This has great significance for us. We have a tendency to see life in terms of what it brings us. In our own country the highly competitive economic system has in it the temptation to "use" people. Love is seen in terms of what we get out of it. This is caricatured by the smiling salesman or the back-slapping politician. It underlies the Dale Carnegie emphasis on developing the personality.

In such an atmosphere there is a real temptation to see people as "things." Those people "count" who can add something to our careers or bank accounts. Industry sees its people in terms of efficiency. Business sees people in terms of dollars. Government sees people in terms of votes. Churches see people in terms of numbers. People see other people in terms of race or nationality or social prestige.

The love of God sees people as individuals. This was evidenced in the ministry of Christ. He spoke to crowds on occasion, but His time was given to individual people. It is an emphasis which needs to be recaptured and relived. With the shift in our country from rural to urban living a highly organizational and institutional form of life has developed. In itself this is not bad. It has brought about a much easier life for the majority of our people. But like every form of society of every age, it has its built-in temptations and dangers.

The impersonal and practical character of contemporary relationships is affecting every area of our lives, every order of God's creation. The marriage bond is accepted under the condition that it will "work," which means that it must satisfy the selfish desires of the individuals involved. Societies are judged wholly in terms of their value to *me*. Races and nationalities are viewed in terms of their threat to *me*. Governments are judged in terms of what they can give *me*. Churches are joined on the basis of their service to *me*.

These are the expressions of man's *eros* when it is more or less propelled by selfish desires, before God's *agape* becomes operative in him. The famous words of the late President Kennedy could be used to describe the Christian's *agapic* love to his neighbor: "Ask not what your country can do for you, but what you can do for your country." Properly understood, the substance of these words, when viewed in the light of *agape,* can be applied by the Christian to every area of life. The Christian is motivated by God's *agape.* He is other-directed, asking what he can do for the other, not what the other can do for him.

Such other-directed love, of course, it is not possible to achieve perfectly in this life. Man's fallen nature persistently clings to the Christian and prevents God's *agape* from controlling his whole life. It is because of this that even other-directed love can become something less than the love that is from God. A man may seem to love his wife unselfishly, but in his devotion to her he may allow her to become the object of his worship, the center around which his whole existence revolves. Similarly, parents may idolize their children. Citizens may allow the state to become their god. Anyone may allow his occupation to become the center of his living.

While such seemingly unselfish devotion to one's loved ones or to one's task in life appears commendable, it may be something less than *agape.* Such devotion may, in fact, be evidence of man's rebellion against the Creator by his substitution of created beings and orders for God. Such complete devotion to any "thing" or any "one" reveals man's attempt to find meaning in life by his own ideas and efforts. It leads to disaster. When the god he worships is taken from him, the center of his existence is gone. He has nothing to live for. A wife or husband dies, and the surviving spouse loses all purpose for living. A man is forced to abandon his job or to retire, and he withers away.

The love which is of God speaks to such idolatry. It calls for a higher allegiance than the worship of this present order of things. It enables a man to fix his hope on what lies beyond. It is on the basis of this prior allegiance to the Creator that man finds meaning and purpose in crea-

55

tion. To live in relationship with the Creator gives a man the balanced perspective he needs for a balanced view of his life in God's world.

Accordingly the Christian man sees his wife as the gift of his Creator. In the same way the Christian wife sees her husband. Parents see their children as God's special loan to them. Christians see their society and their government as gifts of God. They see their occupations as God-given and God-controlled. Because they see God as the One who lovingly takes away, their world does not fall out from under them when they are separated from what has been near and dear to them. Their relationship to the Creator as the Giver of all good gifts enables them to bear the burden of separation. They are convinced that all events in their lives are within His knowledge and care. Nothing can separate them from this love which persists and which pervades their lives.

Such confidence in the love of God is not merely an attitude in man. It is the gift of God. Our love is always less than pure, is always looking for something from God. Even the Christian's prayer life is affected by his perversion of God's *agape*. But in spite of all this, God gives man this perfect love, this *agape*. The true love a Christian has *for* God is always love *from* God. We can love Him only because He loves us. Divine love is a gift through Christ and is offered in the Gospel. It cannot be attained by anyone; it can only be received by faith in the Gospel. It doesn't originate in man; it is simply the Spirit-given response to God's redeeming love in Christ.

This divinely endowed love permeates the Christian's relationship to the world in which he lives. It enables him to see the world of creation as the sphere of God's love. It enables him to see the fruits of the earth and the minerals of the ground and the beauties of nature as the expression of God's *agape*. He sees the goodness of creation. When things in creation appear as evil, this is the result of man's

56

separation from God. The natural disasters of creation cannot be understood. They remain as mysteries for the Christian, but they do not deter him from his conviction that God's love is the governing factor in His world.

Such an understanding of God's world affects the Christian's occupational outlook. Whether he works with the soil or the products of the soil, whether he works outdoors or indoors, whether he works with animate creatures or inanimate, he sees everywhere about him the creating and preserving hand of God's love. His time, his possession, his occupation, his recreation — all these are so many opportunities for responding to the love of the Creator revealed in Jesus Christ.

This applies also to the Christian's relationship to the world of men. He sees all men as the creatures of God's love. He sees people as the crown of God's creative activity, creatures made for fellowship and union with their Creator. He sees people of all races and nationalities as the precious objects of God's holy love.

It is this concern for his fellowmen that occupies the Christian's thoughts and actions. He is not satisfied until all men know their Creator and experience the knowledge of His love. He has a "holy restlessness" for his fellow creatures, no matter who they may be or where they may live. The love of God has brought the Christian into a Father-son relationship with the Creator of the world, and he wants all other men to be delivered from their apartness from the Father and be brought into the holy family of eternal love.

This is the message of the Christian Gospel — that all men may again become brothers in the family of God, who reconciled them to Himself through Christ. There have been many attempts to create brotherhoods apart from Christ. Such brotherhoods are not of God, because they are not the family of the true God. Only in Christ can men recognize God as Father, and only in Him can they

57

call one another brothers. It is sonship with God as He has revealed Himself in Christ that makes for true brotherhood among men.

Such brotherhood is possible. We know its possibility in the fact that God became our Brother — in Christ. Here we see the nature of true brotherhood — a complete giving of self for the neighbor out of the love which comes from God. For those who receive His brotherhood there is one family based on one Baptism, one Spirit, one Father.

This brotherhood of God among men is the church in its proper sense. It is the body which mysteriously binds together all men of all time who receive God's offer of love in Christ. While it is not *of* the world, it is *in* the world. The family of God so pervades the world that it cannot but affect the world. The people of God may look and act like other people. Yet they are different. They have in them the power of God's love, the power that can change the world, the light which can enlighten every man. Through them God would apply to His creation the blessings of the redemption effected by Christ.

GOD'S NEW WORLD

The Christian's new relationship to God in Jesus Christ opens up for him a new world. The old existence is transformed. The old loves are changed by God's love. The old creature is re-created and renewed. The Christian has the promise of experiencing this new existence. By Christian I do not mean a man who tries to make himself new according to the moral pattern set by Jesus Christ. I mean a man who hears God speak to him in Christ, who accepts God's judgment and condemnation, on the one hand, and receives God's love and forgiveness as a free and undeserved gift, on the other. Such a person is living in a new relationship to God. This means also that he is experiencing a new relationship to God's world.

But it must be remembered that this new relationship is still accompanied by the old. The old way of thinking and living still clings to the new life. The Christian lives in a fallen world which is continually trying to pull him away from the new existence promised to him in Christ. With St. Paul he agrees that the good he would do he doesn't do; and the evil that he doesn't want to do he does.

Old World and New World

This is the tension which characterizes the Christian life. Even though he is a new man in Christ, the Christian is also the old man throughout his present existence. It's not that he is partly old and partly new. He is completely new and completely old at one and the same time. This tension within the Christian is the tension between his participation in the kingdom of heaven and his present existence in the kingdom of this world. He participates in the natural orders of creation, yet he also transforms them by virtue of his direct relationship to the Creator.

It is this tension that Jesus spoke of when He said, "I am not come to bring peace but a sword." Christianity does not promise a bed of roses. Nor does it encourage a withdrawal from the world. It involves men in a battle — the battle between God's new life and the demonic forces subverting His creation. St. Paul describes this battle in terms of flesh and spirit. By flesh he means the old existence apart from and opposed to God; by spirit he means the Spirit of God, impelling and motivating in the direction toward God and with God. Left to itself, the flesh is the occasion for the sins against the Law which result from man's sinful separation from his Creator. Original sin, the rupture between Creator and creature, is evidenced in the words and deeds of self-living and self-serving. In several of his writings Paul catalogs these "sins of the flesh," these sins of the old man. His use of the word *flesh* in these lists indicates man in his fallenness, man as part of the "fallen" world.

When St. Paul uses the term "world" in this context,

he is speaking of the world in its alienation from God. He is not saying that God's created world is evil in itself. It has become the scene of man's evil, and it is used for evil purposes. Man's alienation from God has turned the world into a hell of apartness and separation from the Source of its being. In this connection the word "flesh" is used by Paul to refer not merely to man's body, but to his whole being in its apartness from God. His body as well as that which animates his body is affected by his fall. His mind and will and emotions are all the properties of a fallen being.

Man's fall has been brought about by the demonic forces in God's world. They are evident in every one of God's created orders, disturbing His perfect creation and leading men into the hell of separation from the Creator. Against this triumvirate — the devil, the world, and the flesh — the Christian is called upon to battle. This conflict may seem to be a fearful prospect, but it is not a hopeless one. The Christian is charged with the electricity of God's love and the power of His new life. He participates in the resurrection of Christ, His triumph over the demonic forces of delusion and death. Within the Christian lives none less than the Creator and Redeemer of the world, enabling him to fight victoriously.

This relationship with God does not give the Christian leave to become a reckless crusader who imposes his will on men wth hasty judgments and premature action. Although his cause may be right, the Christian needs to act rationally as well as emotionally and willingly. His reason as well as his will has been transformed by the power of Christ. On the other hand, it would seem that most Christians are often not reckless enough. They are inclined to engage in cold calculations when it comes to striking out for the causes of Christ among men. They are quick to count the cost to themselves before they serve the needs of fellowmen. To know what to do and when to do it is a difficult and treacherous thing. To live out our relationship to God with a proper balance between intellect and will and emotion is a gift that comes from God in every new situation and circumstance.

Our relationship as Christians to God's new world would be overwhelming in its complexity were we to allow it to depend on ourselves. But God gives the grace to make it possible. When every situation is viewed in the light of love and the realization of His presence, we can be sure that He will enable us to speak and to act in accord with His will. This might well be the meaning of Christ's promise: "My yoke is easy, and My burden is light."

But our burden is also difficult. If we would follow Christ, we are asked by Him to deny ourselves and take up our cross. — Our response to Christ is one in which we are personally and directly participating. We are not the passive agents of God's love to men. We are *involved*. This will mean sacrifice and suffering. It will mean pain and persecution. For many, also in our day, it has meant mutilation and martyrdom.

God wants no self-appointed martyrs, but He does expect His people in Christ to face the challenges of life honestly and forthrightly. Cowardly compromising in the area of Christian witness is the kind of lukewarmness that is nauseating to God. Real Christianity separates the men from the boys. It exercises the spiritual muscles of commitment to God in every situation in which it finds itself. It seeks not its own, but it speaks and acts in the name and by the power of God.

As Christians we live in this tension between new man and old man. Exactly how we live out this tension cannot be regulated by specific laws of conduct. Our desire is the Law of God. But the application of this Law must be motivated by God's new life and propelled by His perfect love. Christian life is the living out of Christian faith. The two cannot be separated. Our commitment to God and our new relationship to His world are part of His one act of redemption in Christ. Faith without works is non-existent. Faith is always faith which is active in love. St. John reminds us repeatedly that our love to the brother is the evidence that we have passed from death to life.

How does this tension between the old man and the new man work itself out? How is our relationship to the world different when it comes to the daily decisions of life? Where is the difference between Christian and non-Christian in the specific situations of everyday living?

The New World of Nature

Most people enjoy the out-of-doors. While many on their vacations prefer the comforts and conveniences of a cozy cabin to a night in the open, yet the experience of being "close to nature" is still present. In an age when more and more people are surrounded by concrete and steel, by treeless suburbs, by ribbons of roads and masses of men, there seems to be a greater distance between human beings and their Creator. As men congregate in cities which they themselves construct, they often seem to lose sight of the creating activity of God. At vacation time they go to the country, back to the more elemental things of God's creation.

Some of this escaping to the country has become a kind of "religious" experience, a new kind of "back to nature" movement. The woods and lakes become not only a refreshing haven but a religious heaven. God's creation is worshiped as a soothing substitute for man's spiritual emptiness. There often seems to be little difference between the nature lovers and sun worshipers of today and those of ancient times.

The Christian urban dweller goes to the country and often tries, like other suburbanites, to live as far away from the city as he can. He may have good reasons for doing so — family reasons, social reasons, personal reasons. But often his escape to the country takes on a "religious" significance. He becomes part of a cult which gives to country living a kind of spiritual dimension which promises a settled happiness apart from God.

As any suburbanite knows, however, there are problems everywhere. His country home is not heaven. He stands in as great a need of God's help as the "less fortunate" city "captives." He may be closer to nature, but he is not necessarily closer to the Creator.

Part of our difficulty in this age of urbanization lies in our failure to see our cities as God's creation. We have established a false antithesis between the country as God's creation and the city as man's creation. Churches have frequently encouraged such a misunderstanding. They have lamented the exodus of the people of the industrial age from country to city as unwholesome and demoralizing.

The period of adjustment between a rural society and an urban society has been difficult. But the situation can be met only by the realistic acknowledgement that this change, too, is a part of God's shaping of His world. It is time for churches to acknowledge that cities, too, are God's creation.

In fact, our present society has brought about the need for a renewed emphasis on a frequently forgotten aspect of the doctrine of creation: that God carries on His creating activity also through men. Formerly people lived close to the soil, and life was understood in terms of a more direct association with God's creative activity in the raising of crops and cattle. Today, for most people, this creating activity of God seems more removed. But it's there! Through the energies and abilities He gives to men in His world God continues to create. He builds the cities and industries. He is the creating Power behind all of man's genius and inventiveness. "Except the Lord build the city, they labor in vain that build it."

You can see God as Creator, then, wherever you are,

in the city as well as in the country. Your relationship to Him does not depend on green grass and tall trees. Idolatry can be just as prevalent in the mountain as in the metropolis. Babel reveals the possibility of sin in the city, but Eden reveals the reality of sin in the country. Sodom and Gomorrah were evil, but so was the idolatry at the country shrines of Baal throughout Israel. In Christ the believer is offered a new perspective regarding God's creation. God is seen as the living Power behind all of the so-called natural world. This is where the Christian differs from the merely religious man. Both may see the world as basically good, but the Christian is free to enjoy it while the non-Christian is enslaved by it. The Christian views it as the free son of the God who stands beyond it, while the non-Christian attempts to find God and meaning within it.

To illustrate: A Christian and his non-Christian friend are discussing a landscape painting. Both of them may express their impression that this painting reveals the beauties of God's creation. The non-Christian may see God in terms of the landscape. He finds God in what he sees. Accordingly he sees something his mind has deduced. He sees a god but not God. The Christian does not see God in terms of the landscape; he sees the landscape in terms of God. He does not deduce God from the painting. He has come to know God in the revelation of Christ. The picture he sees depicts the handiwork of the God he knows.

This applies to every area of the Christian life in this world. The Christian is a part of God's created order, but he is not enslaved by it. The created world does not determine his idea of God. It does not control his life. He is not hemmed in by his creaturely existence in such a way that he must grope for God and for the goals by which he lives. God has invaded this present life of his. He has accepted God's life, and this relationship with the Creator determines his view of creation.

But even as a Christian he is still tempted to live as

though he were not a Christian. His old nature causes him also to try to formulate his own idea of God apart from God's revelation of Himself. This in turn tempts him to think of God's creation as something apart from God. He is tempted to use God's good creation for the purposes of his old selfish nature.

The tension between this fallen creatureliness and his transformed creatureliness evidences itself in many areas of everyday living. By virtue of his fallenness he is pulled toward the misuse, for example, of his body. The precious gifts of creation are used to the detriment of the great gift of his body. He is tempted to excess in eating, drinking, working, playing, smoking, and other areas of living.

These temptations are as real to the Christian as to one who does not profess the Christian faith. God does not simply remove His people from the temptations of life. He allows these to serve as the tests of faith. Nor does He set down detailed rules for the Christian. He does not put the believer back under the Law by means of a catalog of dos and don'ts. Because individuals and circumstances differ, God does not specify what constitutes gluttony, drunkenness, overwork, overplay, and oversmoking. He allows believers the freedom for which Christ redeemed them and all mankind from the slavery of the Law.

This leaves us with the freedom of responsibility. By our commitment to God it is our responsibility to decide ourselves what constitutes for us the proper balance of eating, drinking, working, playing, and smoking. No church body can presume to legislate in these matters, although the church has the responsibility to warn its people against excess and to encourage moderation in all things except in the love of God.

How, then, do we exercise this responsibility? We begin by reminding ourselves that our bodies are the precious creation of God. In Christ we know our Creator. Anything that we regard to be harmful to the body we will try to avoid and conquer. Since it has been established by medical science that overweight taxes the heart, we shall attempt to conquer that demon, difficult though it may be in this land of plenty. Since we know the results both physical and moral, of excess in the drinking of alcoholic beverages, we shall use these moderately. Since we know that overwork is harmful to our bodies and unfair to our families, we shall allow our relationship to God to help us decide what is proper. Since we know that overexertion or overindulgence in recreational activities may be harmful to people of sedentary occupations, we shall use good judgment and common sense. If we are married, we shall not allow our recreational activities to take us too frequently from our family responsibilities. Neither fishing or golfing widows nor bridge club widowers reveal a proper sense of Christian responsibility on the part of their spouses.

Recent studies on smoking have revealed decidedly harmful effects for the immoderate smoker. The decision to stop smoking or to cut down our smoking is up to each of us. Christianity does not legislate. It has the duty to speak of the harmful effects of immoderate smoking, but it cannot say that moderate smoking is sinful. Each Christian has the duty to keep himself informed on this matter and to act on the basis of his Christ-enlightened reason. He will not exercise his freedom irresponsibly but out of the full recognition that his body is the precious gift of his Creator, who has redeemed him from the sinful abuses of his body.

The Christian knows that excess and immoderation are harmful to the body. When he succumbs to this sin, he is giving in to his old Adam. He is allowing the old man to gain the ascendancy. He becomes enslaved once again to the present order of things, to the "old man." But there is at hand the power to battle this old way. Here is where the Christian differs from the non-Christian. The latter must by his own resolution and determination conquer what he believes to be wrong. He must pull himself up. When he succeeds, he is led to pride. When he fails, he is led to despair.

The Christian commits his problem to God. By hearing God's Law as revealed in Scripture he is brought to a realization of the seriousness of harming God's creation. He hears immoderation condemned by his Creator. This message of Law, however, is *not* what enables him to rise above his old man. The Holy Spirit through the Word of the Gospel makes the victorious love of Christ a present reality among sinful men. This love of Christ becomes the motivation for a man to rise and conquer. In Christ he can do all things because the very power of the Creator Himself is present.

This chapter is entitled "God's New World." Actually the world in itself does not become different. It is the Christian that has become different. Because he is different, he sees the world in a new perspective. "All things become new." What before seemed commonplace and inevitable now takes on a new dimension. The world is seen as the exciting arena of God's creative and saving activity.

It would seem that Christians frequently do not show their excitement over the new discovery which is open to them. Many non-Christians often appear to have a greater appreciation of God's creation than those who claim to be His people. Of all people it is the Christian who ought to be enjoying creation. The first question of the Westminster Shorter Catechism reads: "What is the chief end of man?" The answer is significant: "Man's chief end is to glorify God and to enjoy Him forever." To "enjoy God" means, among other things, to enjoy His creation.

The lack of enjoyment of God's creation on the part of Christians is revealed by frequent lack of interest in the natural sciences and in the arts. Our nation is concerned with the small number of students who are engaging in scientific pursuits. It seems our people are so busy pursuing the dollar that they have little time to enjoy the exciting challenge of exploring God's wonderful universe. It is also a Christian calling to engage in the reverent investigation of God's creation in the natural sciences.

There also appears to be among Christians a frequent lack of interest in the arts. We are a nation of spectators. Not only do we not engage in the arts; we are not even competent to enjoy them. We have become accustomed to hearing others tell us what is "good" or "bad." Here again many non-Christians are far more advanced in the appreciation of God's world than many who profess to know the God of creation. Would it not be a Christian calling to "discover" the balance and harmony and sound of God's creation as available to us in music? Would it not be Christian to "discover" the design and proportion and color of God's creation as available to us in art and architecture?

The church has a real need for people who can see the relationship between God's redemption and His creation. It is the church's continuing task to relate the Christian Gospel to the culture of each succeeding generation. Unless she takes this task seriously, there will be a continuing divorce of her message from that of the sciences and the arts. Every contemporary form of culture must be taken seriously — including contemporary music, art, architecture — if the church expects to communicate the Gospel meaningfully to men.

This does not mean that the arts and sciences must be subjected to the church. The Middle Ages showed the stultifying results of such an arrangement. Although great masterpieces of art and architecture were accomplished during those years, the arts and sciences apparently had a limited view of the doctrine of creation. Christian art was usually considered to be art which portrayed Christian or Biblical characters and events. The same was frequently true of sculpture and architecture.

The church of today has been called to take seriously God's creation as well as His redemption. She has become less "other-worldly," less concerned with saving souls for the future only and more concerned with allowing God's future to affect our present. This emphasis makes God's creation more meaningful. His redeeming activity in Christ has brought us to a greater appreciation of His creating activity. Although in His preaching and ministry Christ Himself emphasized this appreciation for the created world (cf. His parables and miracles), this has often not been appreciated by the church.

Contemporary Christians are beginning to understand that you don't have to paint pictures of Christ to be a Christian artist. Whatever a Christian artist paints is a Christian work of art when it is carried out to the glory of God and the edification of God's people. There is no distinctly "Christian" art or "Christian" music. The believer judges all music and all art also in terms of the extent to which it expresses the goodness of God's creation.

God is active through the concern of Christians for the culture of their times. Through concerned Christians He can speak His judgment upon the smut and the stench of certain forms of American culture, of its art and literature, of its so-called realistic writings, of its so-called scientific approach to life. If Christians are the leaven and the light that Christ says they are, they will be using and developing thir minds and abilities for the betterment of our culture.

When God speaks His judgment of Law, He must also be allowed to speak His Gospel. It is the characteristic of some Christians to speak only Law. They are so busy in condemnation that they have no time for creation. God has chosen to save men through Christians. He has entrusted them with His Gospel. Through them He wants to bring not only the condemning message of His Law but also the positive message of redemption.

Christians are the agents of God's saving activity in Christ while they engage actively in the cultural pursuits of their day. Christians should be setting the standards in the arts and the sciences, not by the imposition of Law but by the example of love. Through them God calls men to repentance and faith. Through Christians God brings men from their alienation to the reconciliation offered in the Word made flesh.

The New World of Men

Not only does the Christian's new perspective in Christ change his view of the world of nature, but it also gives new meaning and a new relationship to the world of men.

Most important is that the Christian sees all men as the creatures of God. The Christian Gospel reveals the real dignity of the human being. In our society there is a prevalent sub-Christian idea about the dignity of man. It goes back to deistic naturalism, and it has received impetus in the 19th-century theories of psychology and education. According to this popular concept man has an inherent dignity and goodness apart from any association with God. Progressive education operated with this assumption for some time. Since Johnny is basically good, education consists in leading out the goodness in him. It has taken several wars and other expressions of the brutality of man, as well as the failure of such educational procedures, to cast doubt on the widespread notion of man's inherent goodness.

But the idea still persists. Political speeches abound with it, and preachers of the old 19th-century liberal tradition are still proclaiming it. To this perversion of the doctrine of man contemporary Biblical theology speaks in judgment. It stresses the Biblical view that man has no dignity apart from God. The creature has no goodness apart from the goodness which God gives.

At the beginning God created man good. The creature was good because he was made for communion with the Creator. That goodness was lost when man used the freedom of this relationship to become a god unto himself. This separation brought with it the loss of goodness and dignity. Man degraded himself by allowing his pride to conquer the image of God in which he was created.

This is the plight of all men. The very presence of law in the world reveals the loss of goodness and perfection in man. Goodness and dignity are not the characteristics of man in his fallenness. They are the gifts of God which have been ungratefully refused and denied. Yet such an understanding of man's apartness from God is not popular. It goes against the grain of man's high estimate of himself. It challenges his pride. It is part of his fallenness that he refuses to recognize that fallenness.

God calls men to a recognition of their plight. He enables them by the message of repentance, expressed in the Old Testament and given its greatest urgency in the New, to see that rebellion which stands between them and their Creator. Full realization of our fallen creaturehood is a matter of revelation. It cannot be effected by rational argument. The recognition of sin is brought about only by Him, by His Holy Spirit.

It is unfortunate that Christian people frequently exempt themselves from the fact of their involvement in sin except in a vague and abstract assent to their being sinners. They tend to condemn others in the name of God and frequently fail to hear God's Word of judgment on themselves. Although regenerated, Christians need to hear God's Law addressing them. God's Law is meant for all people, and Christians, of all people, should know that it is meant for them as well as for others. When Christians hear the Law of God judging them, they know how much their fellow creatures need to hear that same Law. They have come to know the forgiving power of God's Gospel. They want to channel God's Law not only by word but primarily by example.

But such channeling becomes ineffective when it reveals a legalistic motivation. When a man becomes "preachy," he is usually dismissed as a "holy Joe," and his witness is ineffective. He must be willing to be "all things to all men" but to withdraw when those things require him to go against his Christian conscience. To be effective, this withdrawal must be natural, not forced or pretentious. The Christian's life among men is not a forced conformity to God's Law but a spontaneous expression of his freedom to follow the Law. He does "what comes naturally" for him. Since his true nature has been restored in Christ, he is enabled to think and act freely and naturally. But the old man within him is also making his pitch to do what is natural to his perverted nature. The battle is continual between old man and new. The moment the Christian thinks he has won the battle, pride takes over. His old nature rises above the new, and he becomes ineffective as a channel of God's Law to men.

The Christian is also the effective channel of God's Gospel activity. This can never be separated from his function as the agent of God's Law. He is primarily the agent of the Gospel, commissioned by God Himself. Here again, what he does speaks louder than what he says, although what he says is also important. Evidence of the Gospel at work is the Christian's faithful and contented application to the challenge of life. His serenity of being, his maturity of judgment, his obvious concern for others are manifestations of the power by which he lives. Men are not driven to the Gospel of Christ by "preachy" approaches, but they are led by the Christian maturity of men and women whose whole bearing reflects their redemption, their relationship with their Creator.

It is for this reason that the Christian layman may be more effective in the evangelization of the world than the Christian pastor. The layman is not "getting paid" for the witness he gives. He is able to live among men where they are. He wears no label or turned-around collar which puts people on their guard. He works among them in their same occupations. He talks their own language — up to a point. In this highly specialized society of ours it is becoming increasingly necessary for Christian laymen to recognize their place in God's world. The scientist who is a Christian can approach scientists in a way that pastors and theologians are not able to do. The same applies to every occupation in this complex new world. In fact, the concept of *layman* in the church needs to be understood in terms other than what it apparently means to most people.

Every Christian is the agent of God's judging and saving work in the world. Each believer is a part of the *laos tou theou*, the people of God. Every Christian man and woman is a priest to the other and a representative of Christ in the world. The pastor differs from his fellow priests only in the sense that he is called to certain specific tasks of official ministration. His ministry is in no way a substitute for the daily ministry of every Christian in the church and in the world.

The Christian's ministry of Law and Gospel in the world can be properly and effectively carried out only when he understands clearly the relationship between his fellow creatures and the Creator. He must recognize the seriousness of man's separation from God. A realization of the universal plight of all men leads the Christian to use every opportunity before him to be the agent of God's love in Christ. No matter what a Christian's position or occupation in life, he has unlimited opportunities to be a "little Christ" to his fellowmen.

Our difficulty is that we are not open to the opportunities. We are too occupied with our own concerns to see the needs of others. This indifference stems from our old apartness from God. The old man is there tugging us away from what we know to be our task. The old way closes our eyes to men's need and prevents us from being God's agents of reconciliation. The common excuse we give for our indifference is a lack of time. We forget that time, too, has in Christ been reconciled along with the rest of God's creation. All time for the Christian is God's time. All time is opportunity to which God calls us. Our entire lives consist of a series of challenges and opportunities placed there by God for the service of our fellowmen.

Sometimes Christians are inclined to separate service to God from service to men by referring to "church work" as Christian service, leaving the impression that everyday living among men does not involve the service of God. You can serve God only in service to fellowmen. You can reveal your love to God only through your love to others. There is no other way you can give yourself to God except through giving yourself to men. Whatever the Christian does for the least of his fellowmen he does for Christ.

To begin to describe the challenges and opportunities of every occupation would be impossible. Every Christian, if he is open to the needs of his fellowmen, will see more opportunities than he feels adequate to meet. In fact, he *creates* opportunities by his concern for others. He sees every fallen fellow creature as the object of God's redemption in Christ. He has a message, even if not always expressed in words, for every man and every woman of every condition in life — a word of judgment and a word of grace.

The New World of Vocation

The Christian's new world of nature and his new world of men is one world. His realization that God has called him to his task in life enables him to see his relationship to nature and to men in terms of his relationship to God. Since God is the Creator of the world of men as well as the world of nature, both worlds are a part of His one purpose. They are one world.

Yet a distinction between the two is valid and valuable. The Christian Gospel reveals that God's chief concern lies with men. From the beginning man was placed in charge of the world of nature. He was given a rational mind and a conscious will and thereby could enjoy a special relationship to God which is not possible for the rest of His creation. Man was not made to serve creation but to be in charge of it.

In Christ this relationship becomes clear. Through Him men saw marvelous deeds within creation that revealed His concern for men. His miracles were evidences of God's loving relationship to people. They served men in need. He was tempted on several occasions by Satan to perform miracles from false motives, but He refused. Every example of His power within nature was also the revelation of His love for men.

Similarly, the Christian not only enjoys the gifts of God's creation but makes use of them to serve his fellowmen. The health and strength God gives him is spent in the service of others. The talents and abilities entrusted to him by the Creator are developed and enjoyed in the service of others. The time and possessions lent to him are judged in terms of his responsibility to fellowman. Every position in life is seen in its potential as an agency for service to others.

It is part of the natural order of things that man has been given the responsibility and capacity to work. He engages in work not only to maintain his life but also to express his life. His capacity for work helps man realize his true being and purpose.

Like every other order of God's world, the concept of work has been affected by man's apartness from the Creator. Work has come to be viewed by man in terms of necessity rather than privilege. It has taken on the nature of burdensomeness rather than blessedness. It has become a means of serving self rather than serving others. It has taken on the characteristic of a "curse."

In the revelation of God in Christ the proper understanding of work is restored to man. Work is viewed in terms of privilege and service. It is seen as vocation, as God's holy call to a station of service to God and men. Christians are reminded that part of the blessing bestowed on the first man was the privilege of tilling the ground and the challenge to subdue the earth. In the work of his hands man expressed the authority God gave him over His created world. It is in man's work that the world of nature and the world of men are brought together in a unique and meaningful way. Man uses the gifts of nature to serve his fellowmen. This is the Christian concept of work. Every God-pleasing occupation is a call to use one's strength and abilities in such a way that all men can enjoy more fully the abundance of God's creation and the realization of His love. In Christ the curse of work is removed and the joy of service is made possible.

The Christian sees his work as participation in the creating activity of God. The Creator shares with man His rule over the world of nature. He gives man the gift of mind and body with which to subdue the earth and enjoy it. When man exercises the powers of mind and body in harmony with the purposes of the Creator, he is a co-worker with God in the process of creation and preservation.

The fallenness of man has consistently caused him to use his powers in a way contrary to the Creator's purpose. He allows his accomplishments to become his god. He becomes enslaved to the orders of creation over which God has placed him. He worships the work of his hands and the wisdom of his mind. He fails to acknowledge the Creator of his body and mind, the Source of his being.

The Christian worker, too, is caught up in this idolatry because he is a part of the fallen creation. He is exposed to one of two major temptations. He may be tempted to see work *only* in terms of sustaining life, in which case his work becomes a necessary evil and a boring drudgery. On the other hand, he may become so enamored of his work that it becomes a source of idolatry and ceases to be the expression of a life given to God and fellowmen.

Through his relationship to the Creator in Christ the believer is called to a balanced perspective of work as both the sustaining of life and the expression of life. He sees his work as the means of supporting himself and his family, and he sees it as the means of channeling God's creating and saving love to others. His work enables him to fulfill his divine vocation as provider for his household and as colaborer with God in service to all men.

It is the proper view of the relationship between God's lesser creation and His highest creature that gives dignity and meaning to the Christian's occupation and position in life. The Christian views his place and occupation in life as God's call to serve others. In all he does he is aware of his priestly status as the agent of God's forgiving love to men. Especially in the present age of operating machines and pushing buttons it often becomes difficult to recognize purpose in the routines of modern industry and business. Attempts are being made by business and industrial concerns to help the modern employee see the relationship of his function to the overall process and the final product.

The Christian Gospel affords the opportunity for men to see purpose and meaning in a man's station and occupation. The exact relationship of the Gospel to each man's job cannot be precisely spelled out, but the guiding principles are available to every Christian. Basic to the realization of purpose in his occupation is the realization that God has called him to his task to serve people. This will enable him to see his work not only in terms of the end product at his place of employment but in terms of the people with whom he works. Both what he helps create and those with whom he works are involved in his call to the particular station he occupies.

Whatever the Christian's task in the world of nature and the world of men, it is service to God when it is done joyfully in response to God's call. Luther said that the cook in carrying out her station can say to herself, "I am cooking for God." This is the spirit in which the Christian participates in his God-given tasks. Whatever he is called to do, he does it to the glory of God. Every act of labor and service can become an act of response to God. His whole life is a liturgy of worshiping his Creator.

Of course, the tension still exists and always will — the tension between the new man and the old, between the new order of things and the fallen order. The Christian is sinner as well as saint. He lives out his position in life under this continual conflict.

But he is thankful for the conflict, thankful for the power available to him in Christ to escape the slavery of sin and Satan and to be lifted up above a meaningless and purposeless existence. He has a goal for which to fight. He lives in constant anticipation of the fulfillment of that goal. His eyes are fixed on God. On the basis of his certainty that his life is forever united with his Creator, he confidently and courageously carries out his responsibilities as God-given with the conviction that he is God-driven.

LIFE IN GOD'S NEW WORLD

Christian people have frequently been tempted to make an absolute separation between the secular and the sacred. The result has been that the Christian Gospel may seem to have little significance for their everyday existence. Their Sunday morning churchgoing has merely served to take them out of the world for an hour or so instead of equipping them for life in the world.

At the same time Christians are decrying the secularism of the age in which they live. Such moaning and groaning serves little purpose when it is not accompanied by a positive Gospel message. To say that the world is secular is simply to say that the world is the world. The world has always been secular, and it always will be. That is the nature of the world. Yet, as part of the fallen world, men have always sought their salvation within the secular, or worldly, realm. Secularism is a life oriented around the created orders without recognition of the Creator.

The most recent form of secularism in America has been diagnosed by sociologists as "other-directed" living. Men set their social and moral standards according to the standards of their changing society. They purchase things because others have them. They do things because others do them. When the "others" are people of prominence, they are the more apt to influence the "little" people by what they say and do.

This "other-directed" living seems on the surface to give men more freedom than the former "inner-directed" or "tradition-directed" standards of conduct. People seem to be free to choose the standards of their society. But it isn't difficult to see that this supposed freedom is another form of slavery to the world, to the existing order of things. People think they are *free* to do as others do, but before they know it, they find that they don't feel secure unless they are doing what others are doing. They are driven to follow the crowd. Their freedom is their slavery. This is the result of living only within the dimension of the secular. True freedom comes only when a man stands with God in a relationship which can judge the orders of society and transform them.

The Christian is part of the secular realm. Even though he has been raised above it, he also stands within it. He participates in the orders of creation, in the human stations of life. But he participates in them as one who is also a participant in God's spiritual kingdom. This makes his place in the world different from the place of non-Christian man. His existence is not a secular one. Nor is it a purely spiritual one. It is a spiritual-secular existence.

There is a danger in speaking of the Christian's life as participation in two realms. It is the danger of thinking that he leads two lives, one secular and one spiritual.

Martin Luther has been falsely accused of making such a separation, no doubt because some who have misunderstood him have frequently made such a division in their theology and practice. Luther did not suggest a *separation* between the secular and the spiritual but a *distinction*. Such a distinction is important and useful. It serves to show the difference between a life determined by the orders of creation apart from God and a life directed by a relationship with the Creator.

For the Christian there is no absolute division between secular and spiritual. All of God's creation has become sanctified to him. He sees all of life within the natural orders of the world as having been redeemed. His Christian faith pervades all of his present relationships. He is not subjected to the fallen world but lives in the freedom of obedience to the Creator. In the light of His love the Christian evaluates his place in the world and his position in life. By God's Law he is led to see how repeatedly and consistently he fails to channel God's love to others. By God's Gospel he is led to a deeper submission to the power that enables him to channel it more effectively.

In Society

Only through the penetration of the secular realm by the spiritual can the redemption by Christ be effectively brought to bear on the world. Only as the kingdom of God invades the lives of men can they experience freedom in the kingdoms of His world.

Because of the fallenness of God's creatures, His world is filled with antagonism and tension among men. This is true not only of the home but also of the community, the government, and the church. A most crucial tension in our American society is that between the races. Former tensions between the European nationalities who settled our country have been quite well resolved, but tensions between those of European Caucasian stock and people of other-continental backgrounds have seemingly increased.

What is the Christian's responsibility in the present situation? Attitudes vary — all the way from indifferent passivism to indiscriminate activism. The problem is extremely complex. Those who view it merely in terms of North or South, Christian or non-Christian, love or hate simply do not understand the difficulties involved. The Christian is called by his God to think and act in terms of unselfish concern and responsibility. It would seem that the phrase *responsibility in love* ought to be the keyword for Christians on either side of the barrier.

It is evident that irresponsibility has characterized the people of both sides in the racial issue. The white Christian irresponsibly fails to recognize the Negro in terms of an individual created and redeemed by God. Similarly, the Christian Negro has the responsibility of seeing the white man as a fellow-redeemed creature of God. This responsibility of love on both sides includes forgiveness and patience as well as a sensitive conscience and a heart which cares.

The Christian's concern extends to the poor and underprivileged. In our American society the lines between extreme wealth and extreme poverty are diminishing. Job opportunities, equalization of wages, tax scales, and other factors have contributed to a greater uniformity in the American standard of living. That many people are much wealthier than the average person should not disturb us. But every Christian ought to be burdened by the realization that many people in our land of plenty live far below the standard of the so-called typical American.

The Christian has the vocation in his community to battle the slavery of poverty. Especially in Protestantism, the organizational church has frequently become a comfortable society of the privileged. Churches move from slum areas to avoid contamination. Christians neglect to participate in the rehabilitation of blighted areas and in the rehabilitation of blighted lives.

Yet it must be said that church and civic agencies are doing heroic work among people of underprivileged circumstances. Community centers, home visit programs, relief assistance, and other efforts are the result of co-operative church and community agencies. These church and community agencies deserve the active support of every Christian. Through them Christians are helped to fulfill their God-given vocation to be "little Christs" to all men.

There are other forms of bondage in addition to that of poverty. The sick, the shut-ins, the imprisoned, the emotionally disturbed — all of these, besides being physically handicapped, often are prisoners also within the walls of Satan. Although our country has no walls and curtains of political bondage, fallen man is a slave to himself. Some forms of slavery stand above the rest. For some it is gluttony or drunkenness; for others, sexual obsession or dope addiction, pharisaic pride or gossip, greed or thievery, lying or deceiving, loneliness or a complaining spirit, depression or despair. There is no end to the list.

As Christians, it is the responsibility of each of us to help people in their bondage. This is our function as the priests of God, the agents of His Law and Gospel. It begins with the people in our homes and neighborhoods and includes the people in hospitals and institutions.

While all men are in bondage as fallen creatures of God, the Christian is free. His life consists in the continual struggle to exercise his freedom in spite of the sinful nature which continues to plague him. The Christian extends help to others in the realization of his own former bondage. He knows that he is free only because of the grace of God. Such a view of his own situation keeps him from judging others or from offering help from a superior or patronizing stance. In the spirit of Christ he takes his place with the sufferer. To help others he stands where they stand.

Viewing himself as one standing always under God's judgment and grace, the Christian will be an effective instrument of God for helping men rise above the walls of their sins and fears. People will see in him one who is different but whose difference comes naturally and spontaneously. They will confide in him as one who really cares, not as one who is flattered by their coming to him.

This is our vocation in the community in which we live — to reveal to men God's power in our lives. The moment we proudly act as if this power were our own, we cut ourselves off from God's power. Then people see us instead of God. Then they will see our pride instead of God's power, our selfish love instead of God's perfect love.

It is amazing how a Christian housewife, for example, can become a tower of strength to the neighbors in her apartment or her block. Others sense in her a humble freedom which draws them to confide in her and seek her advice. She can help these people because she sees herself as one of them. The words she speaks reveal God's concern. The way she listens is frequently of more significance than what she says. It is because she listens as a fellow sinner before God that she is enabled to speak as His saint. Through her listening and speaking she becomes a channel of hope and help to those who come to her.

It is this same concern that the Christian reveals to those behind the walls of our society. It is this concern that moves him to visit the sick and those in prison. There are innumerable opportunities in every community to visit shut-ins, to serve as volunteers in hospitals or other

85

institutions of mercy, to assist in the rehabilitation of deformed and distorted lives.

If any Christian is bored with life, let him become aware of the needs of suffering humanity about him. If any Christian is dissatisfied with his lot in life, let him look at the lot of others. If any Christian feels persecuted and lonely, let him learn to fill the emptiness and loneliness of others.

In Government

All forms of government are a part of God's order of creation. They are expressions of His rule of law, His kingdom of the left hand. Although governments are the structures of sinful men, yet they are the agencies of God. Christians see the government as God's arm of law and order. It exists because of man's perverseness. If men lived in perfect union with their Creator, no government would be necessary. No law would be required. The kingdom of the Gospel would be fully realized; heaven would be fully present. Governments are good because they are creations of God and exist by his ordination. But they can be used for evil when evil men gain power. Yet all of them are under the lordship of Christ and serve His holy purpose.

The Christian, then, sees government as part of God's economy. He does not separate his life into the secular and the spiritual. He rather distinguishes between government as God's gift under the Law and the kingdom of grace as God's gift under the Gospel. God deals with men in these two ways. He addresses all men through those laws of government which establish justice and maintain order. He speaks to Christians also by the Gospel of Christ. The Law is necessary to keep order in the world and to show man his sin. The Gospel is necessary to rescue man from the condemnation of the Law. Government as such has to do with God's order of creation; the Gospel as such has to do with man's redemption. But God's redemption is able to transform God's creation.

The Christian's vocation as a redeemed citizen is that of allowing his redemption in Christ to enable him to serve his fellowmen through service to the government. In our nation all citizens constitute the government. The organization of the state is a family affair. This is the nature of American democracy.

Like all other forms of government, democracy can become demonic in character. It can easily arrogate the prerogatives of God and rule in defiance of God's will and command. For many Americans democracy has become identified with Christianity in such a way that they have come to feel that the democratic form of rule is the only Christian form of government.

Such a notion reveals a misunderstanding of the Christian Gospel as well as a misapprehension of the function of the state. It is a confusion of the two realms of God's activity among men. Either it ascribes a saving significance to democracy, or it ascribes a legalistic function to the Gospel. It either makes gospel out of government, or Law out of Gospel. Either it makes the government a means of salvation, or it makes the church a means of establishing a visible kingdom on earth.

The two realms must be distinguished and kept in their proper tension. The state must be seen as God's realm of Law. It has no authority from God to become the means of man's spiritual salvation. When it wrongly assumes this authority, it becomes tyrannical. It binds men to itself as the source of their ultimate peace and safety.

Americans are rightly proud of the political freedom they enjoy. This very freedom, however, can become the source of slavery. When people choose to make a religion out of a given form of government, they are making an idol out of an order of God's creation. They are putting government above God. Many political speeches reveal such a tendency, ascribing to the American form of government an inherent goodness and sanctity which it does not have. No form of government is *inherently* good, even as no form of government can presume to offer man *ultimate* peace and salvation.

Yet to the American Christian his government is a precious gift of God. Through the Scriptures he has gained an understanding of his redemption by Christ and on this basis sees his state as the high expression of God's holy Law. And so he is gratefully obedient to it. He pays his taxes, he participates in its elections, he supports it in word and deed. Above all, he recognizes its authority. While the non-Christian sees the government merely in terms of human consent to common law, the Christian sees in this human consent the direction of God. It is this view which prompts him to serve good government and to object to bad government, to laws which conflict with God's Law and his fellowman's welfare. It would seem that Christians do not take as seriously as they might the divine character of government and the divine appointment of its leaders. In many cases Christians have been slow to participate in politics and governmental activity. Such neglect reveals a lack of gratitude to the Creator for His great gift. We are privileged in our country to participate in a very direct way in the affairs of government. It is the Christian's responsibility to do so. He is called by God to serve the state. Through the participation of Christians in government God is able to channel His Word of judgment and His Word of redemption. Through Christ's redemptive love the order of government can be raised from corruption and self-service. Christians can give evidence of their relationship to the Creator in Christ by faithful and loving service to fellowman under the created forms of government.

In the Church

Like government, the institutional church belongs to the secular realm of God's activity. It is a misunderstanding of the two realms to think of the state as the secular realm and the empirical church as the spiritual realm. The church on earth is a created order, and as such it belongs to the secular realm. Like all other orders, in its organizational form it is sinful and corrupt and stands under God's judgment. But it is also redeemed. For the Christian the church is the agent of God through which He speaks not only in terms of Law but primarily in terms of Gospel. Through the church's proclamation of the Gospel carried on through its total ministry and fellowship, the gracious rule of God takes hold of people, and they become new by the work of the Spirit.

The spiritual realm is hidden in the secular realm. The kingdom of God does not come with observation. It is hidden in the kingdoms of this world. It is like the yeast in a loaf of meal, like a grain of mustard seed in the ground. It enters a man's life by the Spirit, without visible force or fanfare. Its coming is as inconspicuous as the coming of God in the Child of Bethlehem.

But the hiddenness of the Kingdom becomes evident to those who have the eyes to see and the ears to hear. It is heard and seen in the words and deeds of Him who spoke and acted in our behalf. In Christ God's summons to His spiritual kingdom is made clear. In Christ His Word is made flesh and His deeds among men are made clear. The inspired Scriptures testify to Christ and His kingdom. Those who receive His revelation of God's presence and love are assured of God's power. They are filled with the Holy Spirit of God and drawn into personal relationship with their Creator.

The church on earth is constituted of those people who profess this relationship with God through faith in the Gospel of Christ. They acknowledge that they have done nothing to effect this relationship. They have come to see that they are by nature apart from God. In His Law they hear themselves judged and condemned. While God has broken into their lives in judgment, He also comes to them in mercy and grace. In His Gospel all people are offered reconciliation with God and the possibility of a new future with Him.

When people come to experience new life in Christ through faith, they become united not only with God but also with all those who stand in the same faith with them. To come into a Father-son relationship with the Creator means to become a part of His family. All who are in Christ are brothers under one Father. This is the only true brotherhood. Every other group which calls itself a brotherhood is such in name only. Brotherhood is possible only where there is a living relationship to the common Father of us all.

Those who live in such relationship with God and one another are known as the body of Christ. They are a living organism, a living expression of the risen and ascended Christ, who fills all His people and all things everywhere with His redeeming presence. Experiencing the very presence and power of God Himself in Christ, the church lives confidently and triumphantly in this fallen world. By their acknowledgment of God's forgiving power through Christ, the church's people become the mighty agents of God's redeeming love. Through their witness God's creation is leavened and permeated. God uses them to shine as lights in a darkened world of apartness from Him. He intends that through their reflection and transmission of His holy love the world may experience reconciliation with Him and thereby the power of a new existence.

In harmony with such a realization of the church's concern for God's creation, it is her duty to speak to the social problems facing our nation as a whole. Where there is injustice to fellowman, the church in her conventions cannot keep silent. Where there is hunger and nakedness, oppression and tyranny, the church must speak in the name of the God of all men.

When she speaks she must act, or her speech becomes hypocrisy. Through programs of world relief, through pronouncements on atheistic oppression, through action against discrimination and intolerance the church reveals her concern as the agent of God's redeeming love. Her action in itself does not redeem, but her active love expresses the powerful redemption by Christ and applies it to people. It reveals the love and concern of Christians for suffering humanity. It reveals the presence of the living Christ in their lives.

For this kind of witness to the world, it is becoming increasingly apparent that the division of Christendom is a serious offense and hindrance. A spirit of ecumenical concern pervades the air. It is unfortunate that fear of Christianity's conquest by the overwhelming heathen religions must be the effecting cause. But the fear can stimulate a new appreciation of God's love. God uses the situation for His purposes. He is calling His people not to forget their differences or to compromise them. He is calling Christians to face up to their differences, to discuss them in brotherly concern and love, to arrive at God-pleasing unity, and to find ways and means of witnessing together, under the Spirit's power, to a fallen and sinful world.

As Christians, we are the channel of God's redemptive love to men. Only through us and our fellow Christians can God's creation be reclaimed. Only through us can the spiritual realm of His all-powerful Gospel pervade the secular realm of His condemning Law. Apart from God in Christ men have no hope. They are religious but do not have God. They struggle but in vain. They fight but without purpose.

We belong to God. We know the Creator's purpose for our lives. We look forward to its fulfillment. We want others to know it too — through us. God would use us that the world He reconciled to Himself in Jesus Christ may recognize Him as Creator and rejoice in His presence.

SUGGESTIONS FOR DISCUSSION

CHAPTER 1

1. Does God reveal Himself to men apart from His coming in Christ?

2. In what sense, if any, is it proper to say that Christianity is the end of religion?

CHAPTER 2

1. In what way is God's creating activity evident to the Christian, and how does it differ from His preserving activity?

2. What is the Christian's relationship to the natural orders?

3. What does the term "natural law" say to the Christian?

CHAPTER 3

1. From what perspective does the Christian view his place in the world?

2. What is the relationship between Jesus Christ and God's creation?

3. How are we tempted in the business of daily living to regard people as "things"?

CHAPTER 4

1. In what way does the Christian's relationship to God in Christ open up a new world to him?

2. How does the tension within the Christian between old man and new man affect his place in God's world?

3. In what ways does modern industry help or hinder the Christian in realizing his vocation in life?

CHAPTER 5

1. How is the Christian Gospel related to community responsibilities?

2. In what way does the Christian message speak to the racial issue?

3. Is the Christian's place in society and government to be thought of mainly in terms of ends or mainly in terms of motivations?

4. How can the ecumenical movement contribute to the realization of the Christian's place in the world?

SUGGESTIONS FOR FURTHER READING

Forell, George W. *Ethics of Decision: An Introduction to Christian Ethics*. Philadelphia: Muhlenberg (Fortress) Press, 1955.

Kraemer, Hendrik. *A Theology of the Laity*. Philadelphia: The Westminster Press, 1960.

Thielicke, Helmut. *Man in God's World*. Trans. John W. Doberstein. New York, Evanston, and London: Harper & Row, 1963.

1.25